# Acknowledgements

This little book would never have been written if I had not been given the privilege of being in Daniel's Den personal development course, created and developed by my coach, pastor and mentor Dr. Dharius Daniels. I could never express how very grateful I am to you following your calling, purpose and assignment, which is such a blessing to so many of us.

I further wish to thank my other coaches and mentors, Shameka Daniels, Pastor Laquonne Holden, Teddy Matthews, Shaun, Gabby, and pastor Marcus Dudley. Thank you all for helping me grow and develop by investing in me and seeing my potential.

I cannot miss thanking my tribe in the Daniel's Den community for their support. We are all there for each other, and it's such a privilege to be a part of our tribe, especially Cindy Chan, for helping to edit my book, and collaborating with my daughter to keep me on track to finish the book.

Thank you, Joanna, for your part in always encouraging me and believing in me, and for all your help with technology and publishing my book. Without your support and help this book would never have reached the printing stage. I owe you so much! You are so precious to us all.

Thank you, dearest Debbie, our disabled bed bound daughter, because your resilience and strength of character are such an example of the power of one more! One more day! One more try! You are always so positive and fighting to get through each and every day, you're an inspiration to so many. Despite totally collapsing with extremely severe M.E. at 13 years old, losing all your hopes and dreams, you never stop putting others first, and your selflessness in totally giving to others is such an example of how we're told to live by Christ Jesus. Your very nature is such a blessing to me and others, and I learn something new from you every day.

I want to express my love and gratitude to my wonderful husband, who has been by my side through so much over the last 41 years. You have put up with so much as I've slowly been healed from my past traumas, and had so many operations, I love you more and deeply every day.
And I send my love to my other children, Samantha and Joseph, in whom I'm so very proud, and to my wonderful grandchildren, who have brought us much laughter and joy.

# Contents

Part 7

Assessment time!

Bible versions referenced:
AMP - The Amplified Version
ESV - English Standard Version
MSG - The Message
NIV - New International Version
NLT - New Living Translation
NKJV - New King James Version

This little book is *from me to you - me sending my love to you* - whoever you are, wherever you are, or whatever you are going through in life. Take heart, take hope, and come on a journey of discovery to a new you that's free from repetitive destructive patterns.

My name is Wendy, and I am very pleased to meet you. I truly am! I vigorously shake your hand and say, "Hi!" I'm just an ordinary soul fighting to survive until now. I found some life secrets to a better way of life.

I bet you want what I wanted. And I'll bet you I am right!
You want a better, happier and more fulfilled life. To feel loved, wanted, valued, appreciated, given a voice, accepted, and free to live the joyful life we all desire to live.

So my new friend, I'm not being flippant, presumptuous or forward, just being my friendly self, always wanting to help another downtrodden lost or broken soul looking for themselves and a voice in this lost world of lonely and hurting souls.

*Love from me to you*!
I hope this little book gives you a lift and inspiration to help you to find some wisdom from your mistakes in life, and go from self-punishment and unkindness to yourself, to a new renewed mindset about you, forgiving yourself, learning to love yourself and becoming a strong welded vessel.

It's time to meet yourself in a new way.

# Part 1

# Foundations

## Day 1: Look at your pocket watch, it's geode time!

I will not excuse the spiritual content because it is my life experiences from being hurt and lost to being found and belonging.

I'm sharing my journey in the hope I can lead you on your journey to healing your soul and finding that inner peace and joy that sets you free to be who you are created to be. It's raw in places because it's my experiences, pain, and happiness. It's how I've survived, found my way, found the truth about who I am and who I am not, found I am not who other people told me I was, and found my path to God.

This book is also a practical journal to work through to a better life, a whole you, and find who you are to help you start your journey of overcoming! This book can be used as the beginning of that journey or to enhance your journey further by reflecting on where you are right now. A jump start or a restart if you've reached a plateau.

God uses all of our trials and hardships, pain, rejections, and betrayals, every aspect of our experiences to help us find Him along that path we call life and to find ourselves and be restored and made whole again in our emotions and mindset.

Every hard time, every trial and every breaking moment can help us if we allow God our creator to enter into our life, our soul, reweld us and re-mould us into a much stronger vessel, becoming a much better version of ourselves than we were before.

Joyce Meyer is an excellent, wonderful, and illustrative teacher. I watched her teach a few years ago, and she gave a perfect illustration using a giant geode, a rock containing crystals. Joyce presented the back of the geode first. It was grey, dull, and boring to look at. There was nothing special about it at all. She said that before we give our life to Christ Jesus, internally we are dull and grey like that geode, but then change happens within us after we have given our life 'to' Christ Jesus, change which at first we can't see.

Jesus downloads ALL of who HE is into us like tiny seeds.
Joyce slowly turned the large geode around, showing that what was hiding deep inside was truly wondrous. The inside was a sparkling bright, pure white edge hugging beautiful purple crystals revealed in all their glory.

She explained that's like us. We start off spiritually dead, dull and grey inside, but when we give our life to serve Christ Jesus, He downloads all the seeds of who He is into us. We start with a white layer that is very thin but thickens and begins to glow as the seeds hidden deep within us start to develop. The beautiful amethyst crystals are like the hidden seeds of what Christ Jesus downloaded into us.

Like a plant that sets its roots first under the soil in the dark, the first sign of new growth we see is the beginnings of a new tree or plant as it sprouts upwards and grows towards the light. Those seeds grow within us by transforming our minds through studying and learning God's Word. As we explore the life book God gave to us, the Bible, He will water those seeds, causing them to germinate.

It is often more effective and life-changing if we do not study word for word, reading the bible from start to finish, but instead read it by topic. Google the subject topic you need help with, like anger, pain, hurt, forgiveness, rejection, betrayal, grief, direction, relationships, and wisdom. There's nothing that we cannot find in the Book of Life.

Proverbs is a treasure trove of wisdom. Read one proverb a day for a month, and it will begin a massive eye-opening shift in your mind. I promise you will not be the same. Stick to this one a day for a month, and you will want to start every month until you've allowed this to transform your way of thinking.

As we grow inwardly, we are slowly transforming from day to day. We think and speak differently. No one sees the change in us, but as we grow and water the seeds deep within us over time, we reach our 'suddenly' moment. Our 'suddenly' moment is when other people begin to wonder what's happened to us to create our changing outward behaviour and even the way we walk because we can find ourselves walking with a smile and calm confidence we didn't have before.

**Slingshot**

*Psalm 97:11 AMP*
[11] Light is sown [like seed] for the righteous and illuminates their path, and [irrepressible] joy [is spread] for the upright in heart [who delight in His favour and protection].

---

Reflection 1:

Reflect and journal your thoughts and feelings.

What type of seeds are you growing?
Who is informing and sowing them? You or others?
Are they positive or negative?

---

## Day 2: From vulnerable me to vulnerable you with love

A journey to a new beginning, a new you, a new rewelded stronger, wiser you awaits my friend.

A new day, a new beginning, a fresh start to being you. The you that you lost growing up and have forgotten that exists.
A set free you! Free to fly out of the cage you feel trapped in or that other people locked you into. Free to fly and become your true free self.

From ashes to a new life!
From the deepest depths of sadness to new joy!
From the valley to the mountain top!

From beneath to on top!
From despair to new hope!
From the old you to the new you!

It's about finding you! Will you accept the free ticket I am offering you for the journey that's waiting? "What journey?" you ask. A ticket for your new journey of investing in yourself, your personal growth, to finding the lost you; to spend some reflection time each day for forty days of transformation and changes in mindset that will hopefully propel you forward.

I've added some scripture verses, your slingshots to speak out loud and meditate upon that day. David, the shepherd in the Bible, used a slingshot to kill Goliath, the giant. David was an expert at using his slingshot against the beasts that would come to attack the sheep he was in charge of. Because of all the years he'd practised using it, he was able to hit Goliath with one stone, his first shot, in the exact spot David knew from experience that would kill the giant. (1 Samuel 17:41-49)

Scripture is the slingshot we can use daily to fight what we can't fight alone and kill the giants in our lives. God's Word is a powerful weapon against the enemy of God's children, those who believe in His Son Jesus Christ and belong to Jesus, and those who have accepted Christ as their Lord and Saviour.

What does the Bible say about the past, change and personal growth?

## Slingshot

*Isaiah 43:18-19 AMP*
[18] "Do not remember the former things, Or ponder the things of the past. [19] Listen carefully, I am about to do a new thing, now it will spring forth; Will you not be aware of it? I will even put a road in the wilderness, Rivers in the desert.

*Hebrews 6:9-11 AMP*
[9] But, beloved, even though we speak to you in this way, we are convinced of better things concerning you, and of things that accompany salvation. [10] For God is not unjust so as to forget your work and the love which you have shown for His name in ministering to [the needs of] the saints (God's people), as you do. [11] And we desire for each one of you to show the same diligence [all the way through] so as to realise and enjoy the full assurance of hope until the end ...

*Philippians 1:9 ESV*

[9] And it is my prayer that your love may abound more and more, with knowledge and all discernment ...

*Matthew 6:33 ESV*
[33] But seek first the kingdom of God and his righteousness, and all these things will be added to you.

---

Reflection 2:

Reflect upon these verses. What verse or verses speak to you and how do they speak to you?

Journal your answers.

# Day 3: The welded vessel

I am not an engineer, and I do not intend to be teaching a lesson about welded vessels or riveted vessels professionally. I am using the image of the differences between the two types of ship construction to illustrate a point.

I found an article explaining the difference between the two, which I found fascinating. A rivet is a cylindrical metal shaft with a head at one end and a tail at the other. This rivet would join two pieces of metal together to form a watertight joint when pushed glowing hot through drilled holes in two pieces of metal. This action took two people, one inside a ship and one outside. Meanwhile, welding fuses two pieces of metal using an external high heat source, melting the pieces where they join and taking one person to do it. Filler is added to the molten metal that cools and forms a strong joint.

From my limited understanding, welding two pieces of metal together in shipbuilding created a much stronger joint that could withstand the pressure from icy water, keeping the metal sheets from the stress on the riveted joints. Please don't yell at me if I'm wrong! This example is just to illustrate my point.

Both shipbuilding methods have pros and cons, and this also depends upon what they are utilised for; the purpose of their use decides the best design.

We are like both types of vessels in the construction process during our spiritual development. We break under certain conditions; some of us are stronger in some situations and circumstances than others because we're all different. The good news is that God can rebuild us. His Word says He can put us back together again because He is the potter, and we are the clay.

## Slingshot

*Isaiah 64:8 AMP*
[8] Yet, O Lord, You are our Father;
We are the clay, and You our Potter,
And we all are the work of Your hand.

God can and will work in and through us despite our human weaknesses, our failings and shortcomings. It doesn't matter if we're in a difficult situation or painful circumstances; God will help us to endure. God doesn't stop there. He doesn't leave us where we are because God can use our experiences and our brokenness through His grace and power, enabling us to comfort and help others. But only if we decide and choose to allow God to work through us.

God never forces us. It's our choice. We can help people even before we're fully healed by sharing our life experiences. I've always found myself being vulnerable and sharing my story, even though it has made me susceptible to verbal attack by some. It was worth it to me because I helped more people than I offended.

God is the potter and we're the clay. God is the master potter. He loves us deeply and desires to help us to heal from the broken places.

Reflection 3:

Reflect upon the pressure points that break you in your life. Here are a few examples to reflect on and journal about:

Is it at work?
Is it family or relationships?
Is it financial pressure?
Or are there any other situations you can think of?

Are you a broken vessel?
What sort of pressure affects you to the breaking point?

If you need healing and remodelling by the Lord, pray for Him to meet you where you are.

# Day 4: Studying God's book of life

You can do a research study by Googling a topic or a reference study using a topical bible. You can also follow good, balanced, and doctrinally correct spiritual teachers on the internet via YouTube. Below, I've listed a few I can recommend today, those whom I follow. If you take the time to listen to them, you cannot fail to grow.

Dr. Dharius Daniels - Change Church - *www.lifechange.org*
Bishop T.D. Jakes - The Potters House - *www.pottershouse.org*
Joyce Meyer - Joyce Meyer Ministries - *www.JoyceMeyer.org*
Keion Henderson - Lighthouse Church - *www.KeionHenderson.com*
Steven Furtick - Elevation Church - *www.elevationchurch.org*
Dr. Charles Stanley - In Touch Ministries - *www.intouch.org*
Rick Warren - *www.saddleback.com*
Pastor Robert Morris - *www.gatewaypeople.com*

You can also purchase a good study bible with study notes to help unpack the lessons taught with easy-to-understand explanations. I love Joyce Meyer's Study Bible, and her *Battlefield of the Mind Bible*.

Dr. Randle Smith's lectures on YouTube called *One Hour One Book* are extremely helpful in unpacking the historical context. I find these very easy to follow. As a dyslexic person, if I can understand and glean new knowledge, I'm sure anyone can.

We need to be careful and wise in what we listen to and take note of so we don't head down rabbit holes of toxic doctrine that do more harm than good. Unhealthy, controlling churches do a lot of damage. I know from personal experience.

When we study by topic or something we need answers about, or an area where we need to grow, we call it reading to feed. God's Word is His spiritual food and nourishment for our souls. As we read to feed on the spiritual food, we discover the nuggets of God's Word, which forever reveal new insights to us. We find we have a changing mindset. We grow in increments, which change our mindset inwardly, and we begin to feel different. But like that geode, no one else can see that inner growth until our 'suddenly' moment.

The time will come when people wonder where this more likeable, kinder, gentler, and happier you come from. They notice the change in you, such as in a crisis when everyone else is stressing out, you take yourself off for a quiet prayer, ask for God's help, and stay calm in a storm. They want to know 'why' you are not stressing out like you used to do. However you change towards a better version of you, people will notice.

## Slingshot

*Romans 12:2 ESV*
[2] Do not be conformed to this world, but be transformed by the renewal of your mind, that by testing you may discern what is the will of God, what is good and acceptable and perfect.

*Ephesians 4:22-24 ESV*
[22] Put off your old self, which belongs to your former manner of life and is corrupt through deceitful desires, [23] and to be renewed in the spirit of your minds, [24] and to put on the new self, created after the likeness of God in true righteousness and holiness.

Reflection 4:

Do you read to feed or just to read?
What difference does reading to feed have on your spiritual growth?
Have you experienced the impact reading to feed has in and on your life?

Reflect and journal your thoughts.

# Day 5: How healthy is your mind, soul, heart and spirit?

When we do our part and study God's Word daily, we become transformed by the renewing of our minds. God's Word feeds our spiritual nature, which is how the transformation happens. It's not a marathon to get through. It's a way of life. Daily! Daily transformation.

As we grow and develop our spiritual seeds, Christ starts to shine from within. God will transform us daily if we allow Him to, desire Him to, and spend the time to develop our relationship with Him. Joyce (Meyer) said, and I agree with her, that if God changed everything that needed changing all at once, it would be far too traumatic and painful. It certainly would have been for me.

I've learned that the hard times and tough times help us to understand the lessons we need to know, and every lesson I've had to learn has always been the hard way. I don't think I have ever learnt anything the easy way in my life. But I am a fighter and survivor of so much. As I look back on every bit of heartbreak, heartache, pain, distress, despair, poverty, loneliness, grief, abuse, rejection, betrayals, excommunication, unwantedness by others I've suffered in every which way possible, I would never change one second of it because it led me to path of my destiny that God has set for me to follow.

A long time ago, I read a book by Jeanne Guyon called *Experiencing the Depths of Jesus Christ*. It took me three months to achieve the meditation exercises in the book's beginning chapters. The essence of what she says is that if we see God as being in control of everything that happens to us in our life, we learn to rest in His arms, to sink back and feel His arms around us, to trust God that all things are part of God's plan for us. We can stay next to God, be calm and rested despite all that's happening around us or to us.

Sometimes, in abusive situations, we cannot just simply say, "Hit me again." This saying does not mean this type of situation. From my own life experiences, I read this as meaning after suffering domestic abuse, sexual abuse, emotional abuse, psychological abuse, broken marriages, etc., that in the end, things will all turn out okay for my good. The bigger picture is not the one we see when things are happening.

Dr. Charles Stanley said in one of his sermons that we might not understand or like what is happening now; it may be uncomfortable, painful, challenging, and scary. We feel bewildered but must say to God, "Well, Lord, I don't like this. It's a bad situation for me right now, but I know You are in this with me and that You have a plan and a purpose for my life, and it's a good one, even if right now, it certainly doesn't feel like it, so I trust You, Lord, that in the end, You will help me to see and understand what this is all about."

I didn't understand 'my' bigger picture, especially about a massively traumatic event in my life and that of my family, and the things that were said, the pain, the hurt, the dramatic things that was happening, the rejections and betrayals, until 12 years later, when I suddenly saw the why of it all.

Every time life breaks us, God is the welder, the riveter, the potter, who puts us back together, and then we become even stronger. We can grow in resilience and wisdom if we trust in God and go to the God to help us, heal us and give us the knowledge we need to help us to forgive those who have hurt us. Then we can come out the other side, not being bitter but better. But, sometimes, we need patience until we see the bigger picture. It's not just us; sometimes, we must wait for life changes in others or let go and move forward. Not bitter, but better for having gone through to the other side.

Did you catch that? Bitter or better! Because we can't be both!

## Slingshot

*Ephesians 4:31 ESV*
[31] Let all bitterness and wrath and anger and clamour and slander be put away from you, along with all malice.

We need to let go of bitterness before it gets a hold on us and how we talk and behave. Bitterness is a killer of our souls. Bitterness stops us from being joyful and happy. Bitterness can make us feel quite ill and can ruin our lives.

Anger as an emotion is not a sin. It becomes sin if we act on our anger. So, learn to let go of anger before you act. It would help if you need to have self-control over your feelings and emotions. Anger is another emotion that can make us become ill if we don't let go of it. If we have anger management issues, we need to seek help in anger management counselling. Conquer this with help.

---

Reflection 5:

Reflect and journal your thoughts.

Have you ever suffered bitterness about something?
How did it affect your health, relationships, and emotions?
Have you had issues with anger?
What were the outcomes? And what have you learnt from them?

---

See the broken parts of your life as something God wants to use to help you become wiser and stronger than before. God is the ultimate healer; He created us in our mother's womb. His Word says that. He loves us, and He wants us to love Him and trust Him. Will you allow Him to be the welder, riveter or the potter of your broken life and the broken you? And for Him to help you to become a strong welded vessel?

## Day 6: Rabbit holes

Here we go; fasten your seat belts, buckle up and hang on!
Your journey of discovery begins!

Let me ask you a question...
Have you ever found yourself down a rabbit hole? I've experienced that many times in my life. I know this phrase is from Lewis Carroll's 1865 classic, *Alice's Adventures in Wonderland,* and I thought I knew what it meant, but I looked it up just in case.

Rabbit Holes:
The first meaning I found was this one:
Noun - This refers to a strange, disorienting, or frustrating situation or experience that is typically difficult to navigate. (www.dictionary.com)

Yes, I've had quite a few highly troubling situations to both cope with and deal with and challenging to navigate.

The second said:
Figurative - Used to indicate passage into a strange, surreal, or nonsensical situation or environment. (www.oed.com)

And yes, I've had experiences and situations I've felt trapped in, as well as some confusing events and conditions that were bizarre. Still there were also many unexpected, beautiful times of being transported spiritually.

There were various other explanations; another one was that it represents the child's struggle to survive in the confusing world of adults. To understand our adult world, Alice has to overcome the open-mindedness characteristic of children. (www.alice-in-wonderland.net)

How did Alice fall into a rabbit hole?

The rabbit pulls out a watch from his waistcoat pocket and runs away across the field and down a hole. Alice impulsively follows the rabbit and tumbles down a steep hole that resembles a well, falling slowly for a long time.

As a child and as an adult, I've been down many rabbit holes, and I can resonate with Alice, as I have also acted impulsively.

## Slingshot

*Romans 12:2 AMP*
[2] And do not be conformed to this world [any longer with its superficial values and customs], but be transformed and progressively changed [as you mature spiritually] by the renewing of your mind [focusing on godly values and ethical attitudes], so that you may prove [for yourselves] what the will of God is, that which is good and acceptable and perfect [in His plan and purpose for you].

□□

Reflection 6:

Reflect and journal your thoughts.

Have you fallen down any rabbit holes?
If so, how?
What did you learn from your tumbles down the rabbit holes?
Have you repeated the same patterns that caused you to tumble?
What will you do differently in the future?

## Part 2

## Pull out your pocket watch! Check the time! Let's get going!

Take your time with this part of the book because it will lay a foundation for understanding yourself. Each exercise may cause some resurfacing of old memories, which may have different degrees of pain for you, cause others to relive joyful memories or a mixture of both.

These old memories were a very emotional and painful part of my journey, but every second of the pain I've been through to reach a new understanding of myself has been worth it. So, if you can stick with the process of uncovering yourself from your past and press on until you're out the other side, you will reap the rewards of your inner work. It took me almost a year of feeling torn apart inside before I was suddenly out the other side. I'd go through it all again if I had to, because the freedom I now feel to be true to my authentic self was worth every ounce of the pain.

To understand why and how we fall into rabbit hole situations in life, we must first unpack ourselves more.

So bear with me, take your time on the reflection exercises, and deeply reflect upon your thoughts and feelings from each one.

The more significant impact following this will come from the tiny amount spent reading the exercise and the longer time in reflecting on your answers.

Are you ready? Let's begin your new understanding of your journey. Let's grow together.

# Day 7: Unpacking childhood

Unpacking me will help to unpack you!

As a child, I found the adult world extremely confusing. Children learn by observing what they see and hear and how adults treat them. I can only share from my own childhood experiences. All parenting styles are different; how we parent our children will differ from how our parents raised us, and other families have varying rules, with different behavioural patterns often handed down from generation to generation.

## Slingshot

We might have had a bad beginning, but our past does not dictate our ending. With God, all things can change; we can change our mindset and look forward to our future by not dwelling on our past.

*Jeremiah 29:11 NIV*
[11] For I know the plans I have for you," declares the Lord, "plans to prosper you and not to harm you, plans to give you hope and a future.

---

Reflection 7:

What were your childhood experiences?
What did you observe, and learn?

Reflect and journal your thoughts.

---

# Day 8: Let's finish unpacking your suitcase

My childhood experiences and observations affected me deeply into my teenage years, as well as into my early work experiences. The insecurities caused by my childhood and all the confusing stuff going on around me have affected me most of my life. I've been too impulsive, running after the wrong romance, falling down a rabbit hole with the wrong man once or twice, and finding myself jumping out of one frying pan only to fall into a new fire. It's taken me until I'm 68 years old to stop falling down the rabbit hole of needing approval or people pleasing and to feel free of needing other people's approval, able to start my journey afresh to be me, free to be me at last. To fly out of my cage and feel truly free.

**Slingshot**

*Isaiah 40:31 ESV*
[31] ...but they who wait for the Lord shall renew their strength; they shall mount up with wings like eagles; they shall run and not be weary; they shall walk and not faint.

God promises to give strength to those of us who feel exhausted by life and its many unexpected trials. God promises to provide us with His supernaturally renewed strength in times of need.

*John 8:32 ESV*
[32] Christ Jesus said, "You shall know the truth, and the truth shall make you free"

Pray for the Holy Spirit to reveal the truth to you; He hears directly from God and speaks to us.

Knowledge is the power to understand; we see the truth and gain a clearer picture when we know things. We can see our way forward, our pathway to a better future. Truth is often painful to embrace, but denial of truth only buries the pain in the short term until the next time history repeats itself. Every time we bury pain, it builds a more rigid shell around the heart, a stone of pain within us. Unaddressed pain creates a sick heart and poor health and affects our happiness, peace and joy. We must find a way to heal the wounds within to achieve the life Jesus died on the cross for us to have: life abundant.

One resource people have shared the healing results from is Denise Bloggs of Living Waters Ministry, who runs an excellent course on healing heart stones. Both online (www.livingwatersministry.com) and as a retreat experience. Amazon also sells her work books.

---

Reflection 8:

Have you ever felt trapped in a cage, boxed in, and unable to be yourself with family, siblings, peers, at work, or in a relationship?

Did you fall into the rabbit hole of needing approval or people-pleasing?

What was the outcome for you?

Reflect and journal your experience and consider some counselling if you need help to move forward.

---

# Day 9: Life experiences

What we experience in our childhood can have a significant impact on us. The things that impacted us as children matter. Sometimes, we don't connect our adult behaviours and patterns with the things that shaped our childhood. We tend to think we've left all that behind us. Unpacking our childhood can often reveal why we do, say, or believe in particular ways.

I joined a program of which my pastor, Dr. Dharius Daniels, was one of the founders. Part of the program took me through exploring my childhood. I found unpacking my childhood extremely painful for all kinds of reasons. Since then, I've been doing a lot more self-investing in my personal growth through Dr. Dharius Daniels' unique growth program, (www.danielsden.com) with a much deeper impact and positive results in myself and my life.

The program centres around four sections of personal growth, and we concentrate on each section one month at a time, with continuous learning from level 1 to higher levels each time we revisit a section. The four cores of learning are spiritual intelligence, leadership intelligence, emotional intelligence and relational intelligence. The emotional and relational intelligence modules have helped me to do some deep work of understanding and unpacking me. I now understand myself so much clearer, and because I now have a clear understanding of myself, I can understand why I fell down the rabbit holes I did, making all the bits of the jigsaw puzzle of my life clearer so I could piece them together.

For instance, if we have volatile parents, it can create an unstable atmosphere in the home. If we are cold shouldered and have love removed as a punishment, and we do not understand what we've done to deserve this or what caused this to happen, it's very confusing for a child and painful too. To be rejected by a parent, especially if we have no understanding of why, can be isolating and cause emotional insecurity. When we have no specified time limit on the punishment of rejection and withdrawal of love and affection, it isn't very comforting for a child because we never know when it will happen again. It can create deep insecurity.

## Slingshot

*1 Peter 2:4-5 NIV*
[4] As you come to him, the living Stone—rejected by humans but chosen by God and precious to him— [5] you also, like living stones, are being built into a spiritual house to be a holy priesthood…. a chosen and precious cornerstone, and the one who trusts in him
will never be put to shame. Now to you who believe, this stone is precious. But to those who do not believe…. "The stone the builders rejected has become the cornerstone, [8] and,
"A stone that causes people to stumble and a rock that makes them fall."

They stumble because they disobey the message—which is also what they were destined for.

As 'you' come to him, (Jesus) the living Stone—rejected by humans but chosen by God and precious to him …. (so too are you precious to God)

No matter how often people reject us or remove their love or affection, God never does. I once heard a preacher say, it's not God who moves; it's us.

Do you feel close to God or far away?

If you feel far away, are you willing to take the steps needed to move closer to God?

Reflection 9:

Have you ever experienced rejection and received the cold shoulder?
Have you ever been left isolated and alone as a child or adult feeling confused, and not knowing why?
Or are you unable to see a way forward?
Were you ever deliberately excluded either in the home as a child, school, or the workplace?

Reflect and journal your thoughts and feelings.

# Day 10: Where do I fit?

As a child trying to make sense of our world we live in, we try to understand where we actually fit into this world. At varying stages of development, this presents different complex questions for us as our understanding and perceptions of the world change.

I did not fit in with my family throughout my childhood. I often felt like an outsider looking in a window, watching what was happening. Even though I was in the same room, I could not join in because I feared rejection and felt I wasn't good enough.

It was an extraordinary feeling, and I understood that I'm not alone in experiencing it.

We might find ourselves with the wrong group of people in our attempts to fit in and gain the feeling we belong or be a part of a group. This decision can cause us to go down rabbit holes we struggle to get out of, it can get us hurt, or into bad habits and bad behaviours.

**Slingshot**

1 Corinthians 1:26-31 MSG
26-31 Take a good look, friends, at who you were when you got called into this life. I don't see many of "the brightest and the best" among you, not many influential, not many from high-society families. Isn't it obvious that God deliberately chose men and women that the culture overlooks and exploits and abuses, chose these "nobodies" to expose the hollow pretensions of the "somebodies"? That makes it quite clear that none of you can get by with blowing your own horn before God. Everything that we have—right thinking and right living, a clean slate

and a fresh start—comes from God by way of Jesus Christ. That's why we have the saying, "If you're going to blow a horn, blow a trumpet for God."

Reflection 10:

Have you ever experienced these situations in your life?
Have you ever felt like you are not good enough? Inferior?
Put down and made to feel small and unseen?
Found yourself in the wrong place, at the wrong time, with the wrong people?

Reflect how this made you feel and journal your experience.

# Day 11: What type of child were you?

As a child, I was timid, incredibly lonely, terrified of doing any wrong, and always frightened of upsetting my parents because I didn't want to incur their wrath. I couldn't read and write properly until I was 11 years old. A friendly headmaster said he was worried for my future when I moved up to the grammar school, so he took the time to teach me. I didn't know I was dyslexic until I was 29 years of age. I struggled to read my very first book not aimed at children when I was 19. I felt so proud of myself reading the whole book, and I remember the awe of getting lost in a story, and how a book could transport me to another world. That's when I became hooked on buying books, and I loved using my imagination as the story unfolded.

**Slingshot**

*Psalm 34:18 AMP*
[18] The Lord is near to the heartbroken and He saves those who are crushed in spirit (contrite in heart, truly sorry for their sin).

---

Reflection 11:

What type of personality did you have as a child?
Were you a brave, adventurous child? A timid child?
A bit of both of these?
As a result of what you were like in your earlier years, how did your personality affect your school experience?

Reflect and journal your memories and thoughts.

---

# Day 12: Confusing world

As a child, I watched those around me have various behaviour patterns I didn't understand. What some adults said seemed not to match what I saw and heard. I remember thinking, 'Hang on a minute, that's not what happened. That's not true at all'. Loud arguments and words had a massive negative impact on me. If we observe arguments and don't see how arguments are resolved, we don't learn how to resolve conflicts ourselves. We can avoid conflict at all costs, often at our own expense. If we observe punishment by cold-shouldering and passive-aggressive behaviour, we can also find ourselves repeating this behaviour pattern in conflicts. If we hear and watch arguments but never hear any constructive conversation about how to resolve them, how can we learn the skill of positive communication, which leads to a healthy outcome for all parties?

I loved my Dad very much, but I soon learnt that there were always two answers for my Dad: the wrong one and his! This perspective impacted me greatly because I looked up to my Dad, and I used to have the same attitude once I found my voice in a relationship. I copied what I'd learned. As children, we were told never to tell a specific person what happened behind closed doors. This comment confused me further as to why we couldn't be open about what happened in our home, especially when it was always to that same person we must not share with.

**Slingshot**

*Proverbs 15:18 AMP*
[18] A hot-tempered man stirs up strife,
But he who is slow to anger and patient calms disputes.

*Colossians 3:21 AMP*

21Fathers, do not provoke or irritate or exasperate your children [with demands that are trivial or unreasonable or humiliating or abusive; nor by favouritism or indifference; treat them tenderly with loving kindness], so they will not lose heart and become discouraged or unmotivated [with their spirits broken].

*1 John 3:18 AMP*

18 Little children (believers, dear ones), let us not love [merely in theory] with word or with tongue [giving lip service to compassion], but in action and in truth [in practice and in sincerity, because practical acts of love are more than words].

---

Reflection 12:

Did you grow up in an unstable, volatile, dysfunctional home or a calm and peaceful home environment?
How did the home and environment you grew up in affect you as a child?

Reflect and journal your thoughts and memories about your upbringing.

---

# Day 13: Impact of childhood

My childhood left me feeling inadequate in several ways, not just because I didn't understand how to deal with conflict. I was a very insecure young adult totally unsure of how to navigate the adult world. I never felt accepted, valued, or worth anything. Being unable to read, write or do maths to any significant level of ability profoundly impacted most of my life. I had very few options to choose from in the workplace. So, escaping my home life, which felt extraordinarily narrow and at times controlling, and wanting to experience freedom, I married my first husband at 17 years old. We moved approximately 70 miles away from the only home I knew and started married life. Later on, my story may come into my writing because I write from my heart and personal experiences. But for now, I shall leave it here.

**Slingshot**

*James 1:5 NIV*
5 If any of you lacks wisdom, you should ask God, who gives generously to all without finding fault, and it will be given to you.

*Romans 12:1-2 MSG*
1-2 So here's what I want you to do, God helping you: Take your everyday, ordinary life—your sleeping, eating, going-to-work, and walking-around life—and place it before God as an offering. Embracing what God does for you is the best thing you can do for him. Don't become so well-adjusted to your culture that you fit into it without even thinking. Instead, fix your attention on God. You'll be changed from the inside out. Readily recognise what he wants from you, and quickly respond to it. Unlike the culture around you, always dragging you down

to its level of immaturity, God brings the best out of you, develops well-formed maturity in you.

Begin studying God's book of life, the Bible. Start with the wisdom in Proverbs and the New Testament book of Ephesians. We learn through experience that God's ways are always the better way to live our life.

*Ephesians 2:19 AMP*
[19] So then you are no longer strangers and aliens [outsiders without rights of citizenship], but you are fellow citizens with the saints (God's people), and are [members] of God's household

You and I have been adopted into God's family and have become God's children.

---

Reflection 13:

How did you feel leaving the home you grew up in? (Whether it's a family home, children's home, foster care, adopted home, stepfamily situations, etc.)

How did your childhood affect you?
Has it held you back, and if so, record this in your journal.
Has it left you any self-limiting belief in yourself or damaged your mindset about how you feel about yourself?

Reflect upon your thoughts and journal them.

---

# Part 3

# That Inner Battleground

# Day 14: Do you believe in yourself?

I never believed in myself, and at 68 years old, I still fight that inner battleground to think I can, rather than can't. As soon as anyone starts teaching me anything new, I hear that old tape in my head. "I can't; I can't, I can't, I don't get it, I don't get it." Then panic sets in, and my brain starts to go into a meltdown, preventing me from hearing what's being said. The panic takes over, tears well up, I get very emotional and ratty, and I give up before I've even started. This emotion and panic started in school when I couldn't grasp what I was being taught. I really wanted to. I loved learning but could not absorb the teaching, no matter how hard I tried.  No one diagnosed me as having dyslexia back then. This experience left me with scars and wounds on the inside and psychological damage because I felt thick, stupid, inadequate, less than others who could, and a deep-seated pain no one could see, but I felt severely every day of my life. School was hell for me every day of my school life. The saying that school days are the best days of your life was a lie for me!

## Slingshot

*Philippians 4:6 NIV*
6 Do not be anxious about anything, but in every situation, by prayer and petition, with thanksgiving, present your requests to God.

*Philippians 4:13 AMP*
13 I can do all things [which He has called me to do] through Him who strengthens and empowers me [to fulfil His purpose—I am self-sufficient in Christ's sufficiency; I am ready for anything and equal to anything through Him who infuses me with inner strength and confident peace.]

Reflection 14:

Reflect on your school days. Were they the best days of your life or the worst?

Have you ever had this experience of panic, not being able to grasp what was being taught?

Do you embrace new learning experiences with joy or dread? Panic or calm?

Reflect upon your thoughts and journal them.

# Day 15: Feeling devalued

All this devaluing of me that I felt growing up, from my feelings within the family, around school teachers and peers, in work situations, etc., led me to fall down many rabbit holes impulsively. It led to broken marriages, allowing myself to be a victim, being abused by men, and suffering such low self-esteem and lack of worth, which in turn caused me to fall down even more rabbit holes as I struggled to feel loved and accepted.

## Slingshot

*Psalm 139:13-14 ESV*
[13] For you formed my inward parts;
you knitted me together in my mother's womb.
[14] I praise you, for I am fearfully and wonderfully made.
Wonderful are your works;
my soul knows it very well.

*Luke 12:7 AMP*
[7] Indeed the very hairs of your head are all numbered. Do not be afraid; you are far more valuable than many sparrows.

*1 Peter 2:4 AMP*
[4] Come to Him [the risen Lord] as to a living Stone which men rejected and threw away, but which is choice and precious in the sight of God.

Reflection 15:

Have you ever felt devalued?
Have you ever felt a lack of self-esteem?
Have you ever been a victim of abuse?

Has it left you feeling angry?
Has it affected your life, and if so, how?
How do you feel about what happened now?
Have you ever felt worthless?
Do you feel accepted for who you are?

Reflect upon your thoughts and journal them.

If this reflection has brought up any trauma from your past or present, please seek out professional counselling, support and help.

# Day 16: Shame

At times, I felt such a sense of shame for all the stuff I had been through. The abuse caused me to feel such guilt and low self-esteem that, at one point, I decided to take my own life. Thankfully, I was interrupted in that plan, and I'm still here to tell the tale.

When we feel a deep sense of shame and we struggle to let go of it, it can become toxic, affecting how we see ourselves, damaging our self-esteem, and confidence.

Many of us have experienced shame at some point, usually when we do something we feel is silly or wrong. I felt the shame of not being able to read and write or do maths at school, which was compounded by toxic shame put onto me by peers at high school. But also, victims of abuse can feel shame for what happened to them. I certainly did. As a child, I was sexually abused twice and quite severely. I shared with an adult I thought was always going to be there for me, only to be told it never happened, even though the last time it happened, the police were involved. They explained what had happened to the adult, and as soon as they had left, I was told, "You must have done something to encourage it." I was left seriously bruised inside, black and purple all over my back, legs and arms, and alone to cope and manage the emotional and mental aftereffects. We may feel shame and humiliation because we've said or shared something that left us vulnerable in front of others. This shame and humiliation can create feelings of insecurity and anxiety causing us to feel a lack of self-worth.

I know I've done things in my past before I knew Jesus as my Lord and Saviour that I seriously wish I hadn't done. But I've learnt to forgive myself and to love myself. I never felt worthy as a child or as an adult until I learnt how much Jesus loves me. And Jesus loves you too. Deeply.

You need to hear that. You are not your past. You are your present and your future. You are who you decide you are, not who others say you are.


**Slingshot**

*Romans 10:11 AMP*
[11] For the Scripture says, "Whoever believes in Him [whoever adheres to, trusts in, and relies on Him] will not be disappointed [in his expectations]."

*Romans 5:5 NIV*
[5] And hope does not put us to shame, because God's love has been poured out into our hearts through the Holy Spirit, who has been given to us.

---

Reflection 16:

Have you ever carried around shame?
Do you need freeing from that feeling of shame?
Have you ever had mental health affecting your life?
Have you ever felt like life was not worth living?

Christine Caine's book about "*Shame*" will genuinely help you here. It is one of the best books I've ever read about shame, how to overcome it.

Reflect upon your thoughts and journal them.

---

# Day 17: Poverty and single motherhood

At one point in my life, I was a single mother of two. I had a few weeks-old baby and a daughter who was just over two years old. I was in abject poverty, homeless, and with no idea where we would live, or how we would get by. My ex-husband would not pay what the court set as the maintenance amount, and I could not get social benefits because he was supposed to be paying me maintenance to feed and clothe the children. I had to solely fight to survive, find a home, get a mortgage, and protect my babies from an abusive man. My family lived about 70 miles away and I couldn't afford to go back there to live. Looking back on it all, I had no idea that my life would turn out like it has. Today I look back at that time and cannot believe how God has blessed me with so much. I am very grateful to the Lord for His provision.

**Slingshot**

*Romans 8:1 NIV*
¹Therefore, there is now no condemnation for those who are in Christ Jesus ...

Romans 8 goes on to explain that once we've been forgiven of our sins, through our confession of them, and giving our lives to serve Jesus Christ, we are set free from our former shame. Read the whole section if you wish in Romans 8:1-17.

*Matthew 6:31- 34 AMP*
³¹Therefore do not worry or be anxious (perpetually uneasy, distracted), saying, 'What are we going to eat?' or 'What are we going to drink?' or 'What are we going to wear?' ³²For the [pagan] Gentiles eagerly seek all these things; [but do not worry,] for your heavenly

Father knows that you need them. [33] But first and most importantly seek (aim at, strive after) His kingdom and His righteousness [His way of doing and being right—the attitude and character of God], and all these things will be given to you also.

[34] "So do not worry about tomorrow; for tomorrow will worry about itself. Each day has enough trouble of its own.

---

Reflection 17:

Have you ever been in poverty?
How did this make you feel?
Have you ever felt like life was always against you?
Have you overcome these times or are you still struggling in life?

Reflect and journal how you either felt in the bad times, or overcame them.

---

# Part 4

# Approval From Others!

# Day 18: People pleasing patterns

Keep moving forwards! Check That Pocket Watch! What Time Is It?

Never Too Late! Keep Moving Onwards!

I am now on a new adventure, and instead of I can't, I'm saying over and over to myself, "Yes I can!"

I'm not giving up. My lifetime on this earth is only going one way, and I'm in the last season of my life, and it's going to be my best ever!

I hope this book will help those of us who feel left out from life, those who've been a victim in any way, those who cannot read well, or feel unwanted, unvalued, shame about their past, lost, shunned by society, those who felt uneducated, have no sense of self-esteem, no confidence or self-worth, to find some encouragement, peace, and a way of believing in yes, instead of no, I can instead of I can't. That's my hope in this journal for you personally.

It is never too late no matter what season of life you're in right now! It's never too late no matter what age you are! It's never too late even if you 'think' it is! It's NEVER too late! So, let's get running!

I have spent most of my life needing others' approval. This has been both damaging and devastating to me. When we need other people's approval, we hand others the power to make us happy or miserable. It's taken a majority of my life to break this pattern. I was brought up to be a compliant child, and always tried so hard to gain approval from those I loved, even as an adult. This was the generational pattern handed down to me. I know that from intimate conversations with my mother as I was growing up and as an adult.

Generational patterns can carry through the family line from one generation to the next that are hard to break free from. For me the journey began when I became a believer in Jesus Christ. And until and unless God comes along and helps us to break free, we can be trapped in generational patterns all our life. I firmly believe this from my experience growing up observing family patterns, and from a wider picture of life in ministry.

This pattern of the compliant child and needing approval of others stopped me from being able to say no! And as Dr. Henry Cloud says, "No!" is a complete sentence in itself. It needs no justifications or explanations. My inability to say no created many situations where I slowly fell down many wrong rabbit holes.

## Slingshot

*Galatians 1:10 ESV*
[10] For am I now seeking the approval of man, or of God? Or am I trying to please man? If I were still trying to please man, I would not be a servant of Christ.

*2 Timothy 2:15 AMP*
[15] Study and do your best to present yourself to God approved, a workman [tested by trial] who has no reason to be ashamed, accurately handling and skilfully teaching the word of truth.

Learning by studying God's Word daily will help us to grow, but we need to have adequately balanced, doctrinally truthful teaching. Never let anyone bully you into anything, or cause you to comply with any teaching they give, or control you through fear of being condemned by not doing as they say. God has given you a free will to choose your path in life. God does not rule us by fear or making us do anything, people do!

My family and I were in a very toxic church once. Women were not allowed to wear trousers and had to wear a hat. There were all sorts of silly rules. The minister was a bully and did not teach the truth of God's Word. God's Word was used to manipulate people. We left because we knew that was not right. If you're in a situation like this, think about finding a new church that has truthful teaching based on the doctrine of God.

---

Reflection 18:

When you were a child, did you find any family or foster care, or adoptive family situations that caused you to take on particular behaviours or thought patterns?

How did this affect you, inform you, teach you, harm you, or encourage you?

Were you confident or insecure because of the way these patterns affected you?

Reflect and journal about your feelings and emotions. Can you see things clearer? If so, how has this new insight and clarity helped you?

If you need help with your progress, or if some issues arise, you might need to discuss these further with a trusted counsellor, and I would encourage you to do so. Healing only comes when we face the traumas we've been through in life.

# Day 19: Flash of insight

I was 42 years old when I had a light bulb moment. I can still remember that sudden moment of clarity as if I were still there living it. It took me until I was 63 years old to reach the point of 'starting' the full journey to break this damaging pattern. But I was 68 years old before total freedom came. And that was the result of pain, hurt, rejection, betrayal, and excommunication from those I love, by those I least expected verbal attacks to come from. I went through 3 years of deep distress, mental anguish, and depression. I had a year of counselling and a long road to recovery. No matter where you are right now, or whatever you're struggling with, or going through, take heart because what God begins, He finishes. Aren't you glad? I am!

I discovered a wonderful preacher who spoke my language, Joyce Meyer. She is a no nonsense, common sense, down to earth and genuinely honest person. She had a very bad start but was able to use her own life struggles to help those of us who struggle with the many issues of life.

Her book *Approval Addiction* was a very good starting point for myself and my husband's journey to freedom from needing the approval of others, or people pleasing to be ourselves as God created us to be.

When I finally understood and grasped from my head to my heart that I only needed God's approval and if I get His approval, I don't need the approval of others, I was on my way to a healthier mindset.

I was able to create boundaries to keep my sanity and gain a healthier emotional state and feel at peace. I felt in control, rather than being controlled by others. Because I had never understood this until Joyce pointed out that allowing myself to 'need' the approval of others to feel happy, meant that others had power over my emotions, not me.

Joyce spoke of the time God said to her very clearly one day during a pity party she was having, "Joyce, you cannot be both powerful and pitiful at the same time."

Wow! That really resonated with me. I have a choice! Me! I have a choice and so do you! So, choose!


## Slingshot

*Psalm 66:10 ESV*
10 For you, O God, have tested us; you have tried us as silver is tried.

*Proverbs 17:3 ESV*
3 The crucible is for silver, and the furnace is for gold, and the Lord tests hearts.

*James 1:2-4 AMP*

2 Consider it nothing but joy, my brothers and sisters, whenever you fall into various trials. 3 Be assured that the testing of your faith [through experience] produces endurance [leading to spiritual maturity, and inner peace]. 4 And let endurance have its perfect result and do a thorough work, so that you may be perfect and completely developed [in your faith], lacking in nothing.

Reflection 19:

Are you an approval or people-pleasing addict?
Do you allow others to decide how you talk, dress, walk or live so you don't offend or upset them?

Think about when this started in your life. What caused this need? Was it childhood conditioning at home? Or were you trying to fit in with your family, school, college, work, etc?

Reflect and journal about your thoughts.

## Day 20: Powerful or pitiful, you can't be both

When I have God's approval, I need none other than that. If I also have my husband's approval and our severely poorly bed-bound daughter's too, then I've hit the jackpot as far as I'm concerned. Anyone else I get approval from is icing on the cake and candles too!

Our quality of life depends upon the information we know. And the information we know decides the quality of the decisions we make. This can affect our life in so many ways.

If you were to ask yourself, do I need the approval of others for how I dress, what job I do, what car I drive, how I speak, and so on, what would your answer be? There are many insidious ways we allow others to affect our quality of life. If we allow others to have the power over our feelings and emotions, then they decide if our day will be a good day or a bad one.

Take back the power over your emotions, make the decision that when people around you want to be miserable, let them be, because there are unhappy people who do not like to see others being happy.

Take back the power over your emotions, and make the decision that from now on you will practise recognising how you are feeling, and stop allowing other people to affect your mind and your heart health.

Don't give the power to other people to control or manipulate you or your emotions. Emotions create feelings, and feelings can cause us to react and say things we later wish we had not done, or behave in ways we regret later.

**Slingshot**

*Colossians 3:23-24 AMP*
[23] Whatever you do [whatever your task may be], work from the soul [that is, put in your very best effort], as [something done] for the Lord and not for men, [24] knowing [with all certainty] that it is from the Lord [not from men] that you will receive the inheritance which is your [greatest] reward. It is the Lord Christ whom you [actually] serve.

If we view everything we do as serving out of our love for God and not for the approval of other people, we will feel satisfied and content with whatever we are doing. It wouldn't matter to us in the same way if we felt unseen by those we are employed by, because we know God sees all we do. When we do what we do as serving God, and we are doing our best whatever the task, we don't feel the pressure to please out of a need for approval.

The best book I've read about approval issues is Joyce Meyers book *Approval Addiction*. This book really opened my eyes and also set both my husband and myself on the road to overcoming this need for pleasing people and approval from anyone but God.

---

Reflection 20:

Who is in the power seat of your life? You or someone else?
Do you need to break free from the need to gain the approval of others?
Who do you feel the need to gain approval from?

Reflect upon these questions and journal your thoughts.

---

## Day 21: God loves you

Even if you don't believe this, He loves you!
Even if you don't feel His love, He does love you!
Even if you don't want His love, He still loves you!

Do you feel loved and accepted by God? If not, why not?
Do you need help to overcome something?

Facing yourself who you really are is often the hardest thing to do, mainly because we all have blind spots. We do, say, or behave in ways we don't and can't see for ourselves.

Sometimes, hanging onto the anger, unforgiveness, resentment or offence that someone has caused us, and the pain of betrayals or rejections and all the emotions and feelings they create, can cause us to focus upon the pain. Our focus on our pain shifts our attention away from the Lord and robs our energy, joy, and peace in life, which evaporates if we only focus on the negatives.

I've had times in my life when others have hurt me, and it's a fight to let go of the pain, especially the last time, as I had a constant reminder of the damage others did daily. Every time our beautiful bed-bound daughter had a seizure after the trauma of someone's words to her, their words and behaviours causing her seizures to return after 12 years of absence, I used to feel the anger rising within me. It caused me such deep pain to see her suffer like this and to see her health rapidly decline so suddenly.

Knowing that every decline brought her quality of life to a new low, I felt so angry at this injustice of the pain inflicted by one person's cruel words. Thankfully, the anger no longer rises, but the sadness remains.

The impact still hits hard, both for our daughter and those of us who watch and care for her every day.

I'm only human. I still feel that anger rising every now and again, especially when others say, "Oh, that's all gone now. You need to let go and move on." Okay, so you've moved on. You're living your life. It never impacted you, but it still affects our daughter and us. It's an insult and rejection of the truth that what happened was unjust and downright cruel, and it doesn't allow us to voice what we genuinely feel. They completely deny the fact because the truth doesn't suit them.

Yes, I have forgiven. Yes, I've moved on. But the reality and the consequences of another person lashing out so callously at our daughter for absolutely no valid reason and so unjustly do rattle my cage. But I've never been bitter. I can say, hand on heart, I've not been bitter and have not reacted out of anger over the situation. And for that, I feel proud of myself because it would be so easy to have done so. And even more so because of the many lies people said about me. But God says no weapon formed against me shall prevail.

God's Word tells us to leave our enemies to Him to deal with, and that's what I did. We're also told to do good to those who oppose us, hate us, hurt us and so on. I tried my best to follow this, and I'm grateful because it helped me not allow bitterness to introduce itself into my heart. I loved those who hurt me, but I won't forget the lesson of not trusting in those people again. That's wisdom!

Wisdom is the life lessons we learn from pain, setbacks, rejections, betrayals, and whatever hits us.

I've never learnt anything the easy way. How about you?

**Slingshot**

*Psalms 36:7 NIV*
[7] How priceless is your unfailing love, O God!
People take refuge in the shadow of your wings.

Reflection 21:

What are the areas you need to work on, or need help in?
Do you have the disease to please, to fit in or feel accepted, wanted, or
needed, at the expense of your own happiness and well-being?

## Day 22: Saying goodbye to shame!

Sometimes, shame holds us back and creates a barrier to experiencing God's deep love for us. I've sure had times of feeling shame way back in my past. Crippling pain about some stuff I did way back, but God removed my shame and gave me a new life, a better life. I felt the weight of my sins and any shame leave me as I gave my life to Christ. It was an amazing experience I will never forget, and I will be forever thankful to Jesus Christ. I've never looked back since that day.

We all have to process pain, neglect, rejection, betrayal, and grief when our health suddenly declines, or the loss of a job, etc. Reflection is a critical component in moving forward. But we can find ourselves being stuck there which is unhealthy. We need to reflect, come to an understanding, let go, and feel we've reached some place of peace within us and move forward.

Reconciliation takes courage and truth. Without full truth, there cannot be a meaningful reconciliation. There cannot be a solid, truthful relationship between people when truth isn't part of the process.

Sometimes we have to reconcile to a resolution that's the best way forward. We have to be able to accept reconciliation isn't going to take place. We can have a relationship that's on a different footing. It may not be the same as the original relationship, and sometimes we may decide to end a relationship because that's the best way forward.

This is more complex within family relationships. In some situations, for our own emotional, psychological, or physical safety, we need to keep relationships at a distance.

Again, I recommend Dr. Henry Cloud's book *Boundaries*.

And Lysa Terkhurst's book *Good Boundaries and Goodbyes*.

Sometimes we can feel distant from God because we believe we are not good enough; we've done too many bad things and feel that we can't be forgiven. We can all be forgiven of any wrongdoing. God's Word tells us we can all be forgiven. God will not remove the consequences of our actions, but He will forgive us if we're fully remorseful, and humbly come to God and ask Him for forgiveness.

God's Word tells us that there is no condemnation for those who belong to His Son Jesus Christ.

Study what God's Word says about His love for us and about His approval. Seek His help in the areas you feel weak in. And find other helpful tools to set you free from the need to gain people's approval.

Read Joyce Meyer's book on *Approval Addiction*.

Read the book - *Disease to Please, Curing the People Pleasing Syndrome* by Harriet Braiker.

Read Dr. Henry Cloud's *Necessary Endings*

Lookup Dr. Henry Cloud's YouTube videos on this subject and join his internet help group.

I asked you to reflect first because sometimes when we do not feel approved of as a child, it affects the way we 'think' about the world we are in, and how God sees us.

Sometimes getting to know the Lord first sets us free from the addictive need for approval from others, and sometimes it doesn't. So, we need the right tools to help set us free.

Sometimes receiving a fresh understanding about approval addiction and people pleasing brings the healing we needed to truly understand how much God loves and cares for us.

And fresh understanding can come from the help of tools like Joyce Meyer's book and Dr. Henry Cloud's teachings.

**Slingshot**

*1 John 4:9-10 NIV*
[9] This is how God showed his love among us: He sent his one and only Son into the world that we might live through him. [10] This is love: not that we loved God, but that he loved us and sent his Son as an atoning sacrifice for our sins.

*1 John 4:16 NIV*
[16] And so we know and rely on the love God has for us.

---

Reflection 22:

Do you know your blind spots? Ask someone you trust to tell you what they think your blind spots are. Never ask anyone you can't trust to be kind and honest and have your best interests at heart, as that could be a damaging negative experience instead of a helpful part of your journey.

Reflect and journal your answers.

---

# Day 23: Hurt Numbing

I remember Joyce Meyer saying people who are hurting can hurt other people.

I know that I've had times in my life when I've suffered so much emotionally that I've felt devoid of any feelings, and numb! And every time it's been from the best intentions of trying to help other people, from people I knew, to my offspring in their teens, family members, work colleagues, and people in churches where my husband and I were serving in our ministry.

We can try to help others, but we need to recognise we can't help or heal everybody. Sometimes helping others causes us real heart numbing pain because we end up being hurt and damaged by trying to help other people.

And yes, damaged people need love and acceptance of where they're at, but allowing them to damage us, doesn't help them or us. As my pastor, coach and mentor Dr. Dharius Daniels says, not everybody's needs are our responsibility to fix or help, only those we are assigned to help. As a young Christian I wanted to fix everybody and help everybody, but I learnt I cannot fix or help everyone, and I learnt this lesson the hard way, the way I seem to learn every lesson in life.

When I understood that God created me to be a unique individual, and that He fashioned me the way I am for a special reason and for a special task and assignment, I was overwhelmed by that revelation. I felt very small and humbled. To discover that He has a set assignment for me, and that nothing in life I have been through, suffered, experienced or learned would be wasted. The revelation that He, God, has a reason for creating me, that I am here for a purpose, helped me to understand my journey towards my destiny with fresh insight.

We are all created unique and special in God's eyes. He has a plan for our life and it's a good plan. In my past, during the extreme suffering, pain, anguish, fear, despair, abuse, loneliness, depression, and near breakdown through unseen, unexpected life events, I didn't know God could be my close friend. I didn't have that insight back then, or the knowledge that God has a good plan for my life. I didn't know God could take my past and use my life experiences to reshape my future, enabling me to help other people to understand their painful and damaging experiences in their lives. And if the people I was privileged to help felt that they wanted to know God in a personal way, and come to Him through Christ His Son, that they too could choose to be helped and healed by God. That they too could choose to believe in Jesus Christ, and like me, at last begin to see and understand the why of things. There's a famous quote by Soren Kierkegaard, "Life can only be understood backwards; but it must be lived forwards."

Dr. Dharius Daniels taught in the personal growth program I am privileged to be a part of that the quality of our lives is dependent upon the quality of our choices. And the quality of our choices is dependent upon the quality of information we know. This statement struck a chord in me.

I had made bad choices, and I have made many bad decisions in my past which caused me so much pain and heartache. I could have avoided these pains and heartaches if I'd had better information about how to manage relationships, if I had valued myself, known that God created me to be me, that God valued me, loved me, accepted me, that I am worthy of respect and being loved. I didn't know that God loved me so much and cared about me so deeply. I'd never been told this so I'd never even thought about God in this way before.

By 68 years old with my experiences of life, I've discovered that this is very true. Many extremely painful and confusing events have happened. Some were quite scary. There were betrayals that I never saw coming, painful rejections, and being stabbed in the back by those who turned against me, especially by those who I never expected would, yet did. But looking back, I do understand the bigger picture of God's design for my life.

Now I can thank and praise God for them all because finally I'm free to be me.


## Slingshot

*Isaiah 43:18-19 NKJV*
[18] "Do not remember the former things,
Nor consider the things of old.
[19] Behold, I will do a new thing,
Now it shall spring forth;
Shall you not know it?
I will even make a road in the wilderness
And rivers in the desert.

Joining a personal growth program was the best thing I've ever done. Especially the one I belong to because it's so rounded, balanced, and complete. I've gained so much insight about who I am and why I am like this, what my purpose is in life, and have worked through so many of my past damaging experiences that created heart stones of unsealed pain. I've grown in every aspect of my life which encompass my spiritual, emotional, relational, and leadership intelligence. And as my coach and mentor teaches us, even if we don't think that we're in a position of leadership, we are the leader of ourselves. We need to lead ourselves well before we can lead others well.

I'm a part of a wonderful group of people from all over the world who thinks the same way. This is my community and family of support, advice, and learning. It's a respectful, caring and encouraging group of incredible people.

If you're interested in investing in your own personal growth, you could also join - info@danielsden.com

Reflection 23:

Reflect and journal about those who have hurt you, rejected or betrayed you.
Were they themselves hurting from something in their lives?
How did you react?
How did you feel?
What have you learnt from those experiences?
How have you grown personally from that time?
Have you forgiven and moved on and forwards?
Are you at that place of fresh understanding?
Or are you still angry and if so, have you allowed anger to become bitterness?
Can you now reflect and see where you either need to grow to move forwards or let go?

A few quotes to reflect upon.

"Letting go doesn't mean that you don't care about someone anymore. It's just realising that the only person you really have control over is yourself." Deborah Reber

"The more we let God take us over, the more truly ourselves we become – because He made us." C. S. Lewis

"Let God have your life; He can do more with it than you can." Dwight L. Moody

"Getting over a painful experience is much like crossing monkey bars. You have to let go at some point in order to move forward." C. S. Lewis

# Part 5

# The black hole of pain

# Day 24: Pain is the way to the other side

Make sure your pocket watch is tucked into your pocket nice and safe. Let's plunge into the black hole of pain, because on the other side of pain we can find freedom and joy.

This plunge is a challenge and a way forward to a better life, but first we must face the pain of finding our way.

I make absolutely no apologies for adding this section. This was the very beginning of a good life for me *but* the pain came first. By this time in my life, due to poverty, lack of food, and surviving on milky coffee, Ovaltine and the odd sparse meal, soup from vegetable peelings with a few red lentils chucked in, I weighed in at 6 stones. I had to feed my baby and toddler first and pay bills to keep the roof over our heads. This meant I often went for a few days without a meal to feed my baby and toddler.

I sat alone, shivering, wrapped up in a blanket in the dark in the tiny kitchen of my very small house, utterly freezing due to not being able to purchase any more coal to light the fire.
I felt totally alone. Utterly alone! Abandoned again! I was truly in the gutter of life feeling defeated, lost, and desperate once again. I had tablets in my right hand and a glass of cold water in my left. I perused the posh cut glass, the one my ex had once been given. With glazed eyes, I was lost and mesmerised by the intricate shapes that an expert in glassware had hand crafted years before.

I was cold and shivering but not aware. Yet another cold winter day, the coal fire embers were dead as the heat had left the fire hours ago. I was unable to top it up. All my coal was gone. No money, no fire. It was dead just like my emotions were. All the warmth of life had been drained out of me. I felt dead, yet here I was, still sitting in this world but not living on the inside. I wanted to die like that fire, be no more like that fire. Can someone please come and snuff out the last of me?

Two days before this the last man in my so-called romantic life had suddenly abandoned me, unexpectedly, out of the blue, just like that! Upped and left! Boxing Day! Huh! What a Christmas! What a present eh? Run off, coward, just like that, running away while I was supposed to be at the cinema with my little girls, their Christmas treat, but it was cancelled. So, I went home and arrived just as he was leaving. With his bag in his hand, he said, "I'm leaving! My son ran away from home, he's not coping with me being here, so I'm leaving you!" And he calmly walked out of my life. Just like that!

Okay, I could have coped with that, but for him to try and leave while I was out? All cowardly like that? Without any apology? There was no sign of any emotion about leaving me and the girls at all; no "I'm coming back later, we can talk about this later, see you tomorrow." Nothing!

I beat the cushions in the settee with my fist, a hard ball of anger expressing and releasing the immense pain screaming within me. I wanted to scream out loud and wail out my pain but I couldn't do that because it would frighten my girls and my lovely elderly neighbour. Abandoned! Again! The quiet sobs came and lasted for hours as my crumpled form slumped across the settee until daylight.

As I slowly raised my defeated body to force myself to put the kettle on, I was thankful the girls were still asleep. I certainly could not afford to wake them up by screaming and scaring them. They'd already been through enough abandonment. At least my baby, the youngest, was unaware of the totality of my desperate situation of poverty and all the suffering I had endured. Her sibling was still a toddler. She too had endured abuse and suffering from the abandonment of her biological father. It was good riddance of their father I thought. His mistress was very welcome to him, the woman who knew I was pregnant, who knowingly waited and then ran off with him as soon as my baby was born. You're welcome dear I thought to myself, at least we're (me and my girls) free from further abuse and his wanderlust.

I'd beaten that cushion to its death! I got my anger out. My fist was my tool of choice to bash the living daylights out of it, the pain, my screams, my anguish, the feeling of the inner death of myself. I beat that cushion for over two hours. Yes, it took that long to totally exhaust myself. I collapsed and my head fell on that cushion for the rest of that night. But when daylight came, I threw out that cushion and everything else connected to the latest man to leave. It was Boxing Day, but Christmas was over for me. I tore down all the decorations, released the chickens we kept, and cut up the Christmas tree.

## Slingshot

*Deuteronomy 31:6 ESV*
[6] Be strong and courageous. Do not fear or be in dread of them, for it is the Lord your God who goes with you. He will not leave you or forsake you."

*Deuteronomy 31:8 ESV*
[8] It is the Lord who goes before you. He will be with you; he will not leave you or forsake you. Do not fear or be dismayed."

*Joshua 1:5 ESV*

[5] No man shall be able to stand before you all the days of your life. Just as I was with Moses, so I will be with you. I will not leave you or forsake you.

*Joshua 1:9 ESV*
[9] Have I not commanded you? Be strong and courageous. Do not be frightened, and do not be dismayed, for the Lord your God is with you wherever you go."

*1 Peter 5:7 ESV*
[7] Casting all your anxieties on him, because he cares for you.

---

Reflection 24:

Have you ever been in a situation of the following:
Have you ever felt abandoned?
Have you ever been betrayed?
Have you ever been rejected?
How did you feel?
How did you react?
How did what you felt impact you?

Reflect upon your life and journal your feelings.

---

Yes, life happens to all of us, and we can't see around the corner to see what's coming. That's a good thing I've discovered. I could have gone under and drowned so many times. But I now know that whatever happens, I can lean on, trust in, and rely upon God to help me, support me, and provide for me. I've learnt wisdom and so much from the experiences in life whether they're good or bad experiences. And even if it sounds stupid to some people, I've learnt to be grateful for them all.

# Day 25: Suicide almost took me for good

Two days later, I sat looking at the pile of sleeping tablets. Back in those days, sleeping tablets were the sort that you could overdose on. My brother was an intensive care nurse. He told me I wouldn't have come back from taking three, and I had thirty tablets staring up at me.

What had I done to deserve all the abuse I had suffered in life? Why me? Was I just useless at this sex thing? Was I not adequate at this stuff? My first hubby couldn't or didn't want to bother. Was it me? Was I that repulsive? My second hubby was a really nasty abusive piece of work towards me. He repeatedly told me I'm not perverted enough for him! He was cruel, constantly degrading me, insulting me, verbally comparing me to his other lovers in his life, demanding, and finding me pathetic in comparison. I've been compliant to the men that came along in my life. Is that my fault? Did I invite abuse? Why? I worked hard at being a good wife: I cooked and cleaned, ironed, kept the garden tidy and went to work to contribute to the bills, except when I had a baby and couldn't work. I couldn't because I was married to a man who wasn't supportive enough for me to go back to work. All I ever wanted in life was to be loved and cared for, appreciated, respected, and cherished. Don't we all need that? Isn't that enough? I repeatedly told myself there's got to be something wrong with me. It must be me. If it's not me, why can't my relationships work out?

I decided it definitely had to be me. The world would be better off without me. I'm not worth loving. Life wasn't worth carrying on living. The pain of rejection, betrayal and abandonment, never being good enough, always found lacking, and all the verbal, emotional, physical and sexual abuse meant I had no self-esteem, and no self-worth. The pain I felt was so deep, so real, crippling, cutting, and so intense that I just wanted it gone!

Even my beautiful babies sleeping soundly in their beds could not take away the intense pain of rejection and abandonment that tormented me. The love I felt for them and their beautiful smiles could not erase the hurt. The pain and the feeling of loss of myself was unbearable. I told myself that they'd be far better off without me.

I no longer knew who I was. I'd lost the inner me somewhere along the way. I felt everything was my fault because I was repeatedly told that from the abusive men in my life. Also, some statements said to me by my own parents over the years, fed that same message. I still remember the sting from some things said to me by my parents and it made me feel I had nowhere to run to for any safety. When your father says to you, "You've made your bed, you can go and lie on it." Where do you go for support? I felt I had made another huge mistake that was costing me dearly and that I literally had nowhere to go to escape.

I now understand that abusive people, especially narcissists will invalidate the truth to validate the lies. (Dr. Henry Cloud teaches about narcissistic people.)

This means that we find ourselves questioning our own sanity. We think, did that happen? Did they say that? Did they do that? Did they mean that? And we lose who we are and start believing we are who they, the abusive person, says we are. We can even find ourselves making excuses to other people who notice things and question us about what's going on, to cover up for our abusive partner.

The most abusive husband, I unfortunately had, would delight in embarrassing me especially to my parents. He loved that sense of control over my emotions. To others, he would act as though he was my knight in shining armour, while all the time he was the total opposite.

What I didn't know until a few years later, was that he'd propositioned himself to my mother for sex, while she was next to my sleeping father in her bedroom. Or, that when my mother came to look after my beautiful eldest daughter while I was in hospital recovering from the birth of my second beautiful daughter, and she was sleeping in the spare single bed in my daughter's bedroom, he jumped naked into bed with my mother. My mother shot out the other side of the bed in terror and shock.

This type of narcissistic person is also a sexual predator and a real danger to women. His charm covered up who he was. I fell for it and became trapped, believing I had nowhere to go. I felt stuck. It was my determination to protect my daughters at any cost to me that gave me the strength to decide to fight back and cope alone. Alone was better than putting my daughters into danger from abuse.

Thankfully, I didn't take my life. Why? What stopped me was a voice speaking to me in my tiny kitchen as a storm was raging within me and also outside, as the wind blew, the rain lashing it against the windows.

The voice spoke loudly and clearly but at the same time soft and gentle. I thought I really had lost the plot. I shot a scared look around the dark kitchen, how on earth did anyone get in here while I was sat opposite the door? There right behind where I'd been beating the settee, was a ball of bright light, shining, and glowing, swaying right where it had appeared half way between the stairs and the kitchen sink.

The light coming from that bright light was so powerful I couldn't look at it, and the voice started to talk to me.

"I don't want you to end your life, Wendy. Those girls need you. They need your protection, love and care. If you do this, he will get custody of those girls, and you must be there to protect them."

Then the ball of luminous light moved towards me. I wasn't scared. I felt at peace. I felt calm. And I felt the light pressure of hands on my head as a red-hot heat flooded my whole being.

Then it was gone as fast as it came. Vamoose! It disappeared!

I went to bed in total wonderment of that experience. This was the second time I had heard the audible voice of God. The first time I wasn't in this house. I was at the big house on the posh street I lived on with my abusive ex-husband. I was in fear for my life: I had gone to bed with a carving knife under my pillow, and a wardrobe pushed up to the bedroom door. I'd pulled my youngest baby's cot into the bedroom where my toddler slept, and taken everything I'd need for the night to feed my baby, including a bucket to pee in, the kettle to heat the baby's milk, juice for my toddler, nappies, and the lot.

I was expecting a beating and much worse when my then husband came home. He'd rang me up and told me what he was going to do to me if he couldn't find a prostitute, and it was the worst I'd been threatened with so far.

I had prayed to Jesus for the first time in years. And that same ball of luminous light came into the room, and I felt hands on my head. I knew it was Jesus, I just knew it was Him. That same heat I felt the second time hit me that first time that night. That same wonderment of how did that appear in the room and where from? But I knew afterwards it was an answer to my prayers. I just knew in my soul and my spirit it was Jesus. I don't know how I did, but I did.

In the morning, I got up and opened the bedroom door, and for the first time in a very long time, I felt no fear. When my ex-husband did appear in the kitchen and he threatened me, I felt no fear. As if by magic, he visibly deflated. He couldn't get his power fix that day. I could see it in his eyes, just as he saw the total absence of fear in my eyes. He had no joy of tormenting me and playing his cruel power games, so he upped and left for the day.

I was so shocked by the outcome. It felt so strange to be free of the fear of his next move. It was like living in a dream. The last time he'd grabbed my neck and lifted me off the floor, I thought I was going to die. And I was so sure I'd get more of the same to come. When it didn't happen, it was like wow! What just happened?

Because I'd been in the presence of Jesus the night before, because I cried out to Him for help, I felt no fear. So, my abusive ex-husband felt no pleasure or power in the way he'd previously gained over me, and he dropped me to the floor and never did that again.

When our abuser loses the power they've had over us, they feel deeply confused, lost as to why. I've found this can alleviate the situation, or exacerbate it as they change tactics. So be aware that an abuser or narcissistic person doesn't always change for the better. They could just be waiting for a more opportune time to strike and use different tactics. Remember Jesus loves you even if you're unaware of this, or do not know Him yet. Your life can begin in a new and better way like mine did all those 40 years ago.

In your pain, fear, desperation, anxiety, or whatever your need is, know that if you cry out to God, ask in the mighty name of Jesus, His Son, He will respond to your cry in some way, shape or form. Even if the response isn't instant, Jesus hears us when we cry out to Him.

Jesus cares about you. He sees you even if you don't yet know or believe in Him. He died on the cross, a painful death, the one and only sacrifice that could save us all from our sins, and to be able to forgive you your sins too. If you were the only person living, Jesus would still have died to save you. Yes you! And to give you the gift of salvation and eternal life with Him in heaven after life on this earth. I do hope and pray you come to know Jesus as your saviour, Lord, and your friend.

I send you my love, I send you my prayers, because I've written this little book because Jesus led me to do so. And my prayers are with this little book. Jesus knows you're reading it, and I filled this book with prayer as I've written it just for people who need to read this book, and asked that they will be set free to a happier, joy filled life. I pray that is you and your experience.

**Slingshot**

*Psalm 17:8-10 NIV*
[8] Keep me as the apple of your eye; hide me in the shadow of your wings [9] from the wicked who are out to destroy me, from my mortal enemies who surround me. [10] They close up their callous hearts, and their mouths speak with arrogance.

*Psalm 23:1-7 NIV*
[1] The Lord is my shepherd, I lack nothing. [2] He makes me lie down in green pastures, he leads me beside quiet waters, [3] he refreshes my soul. He guides me along the right paths for his name's sake. [4] Even though I walk through the darkest valley, I will fear no evil, for you are with me; your rod and your staff, they comfort me. [5] You prepare a table before

me in the presence of my enemies. You anoint my head with oil; my cup overflows. [6] Surely your goodness and love will follow me all the days of my life, [7] and I will dwell in the house of the Lord forever.

---

Reflection 25:

Reflect on your life, have you ever suffered domestic violence?
How did you feel, or how do you feel, if you're still in that situation?
Do you need to reach out for help?

Do not use any device online or your phone if you are in a situation where your devices could be monitored.

If it's too dangerous to ring or email because your abuser is checking your phone or emails, try to keep a journal of events so you have a record of the dates and times of what happened. You can use that in court later on if you need to. But obviously hide it well, and even pass notes of the events to a very trusted person, someone who can keep them safe for you. But whatever you do, keep you safe and don't trust just anyone.

If you feel you are in a dangerous situation, create a plan of escape should you need one. Get yourself prepared and know exactly what your plan of escape will be.

24 hr refuge for the Domestic violence helpline:
0808 2000 247

This is the current number to ring in the UK at the time of me writing the book.

# Day 26: New life! New journey!

The first step for me was coming to the understanding that although I had always believed in God and that He existed, I did not know I needed a personal relationship with Jesus Christ and that I could be close to Him as my Lord and Saviour, and friend, and that I could receive forgiveness and eternal life to come from Jesus, once I become an heir of Christ.

My personal relationship with Christ literally saved me, He saved me, and not only that He gave me a better future life than I could ever have imagined.

I didn't understand that I needed a personal relationship with Jesus to help me actually get to know and connect with God on a daily basis. It's such a beautiful relationship and so precious to me to be able to connect with God whenever I want or need to, and the knowledge that He is with me all the time in all I do is a real joy and such comfort and help in times of crisis. I was 29 yrs old at that stage of my life, a single mother, desperate, lonely, in abject poverty and so damaged by life, I'd lost all my trust in men and I was a mess and in the gutter of life.

Thankfully God sent a very brave lady who invited me to a community bible study. At the time my answer wasn't very edifying. Nevertheless, something compelled me to go. The brave lady became my mother-in-law. I never saw that coming! My life changed and turned round and in the most amazing ways after I committed my life to serve Jesus Christ.

I still had issues and lots of problems to solve, but from now on I was never alone in them. And after 40yrs of walking with Jesus as my friend, my Saviour and my Lord, my life is unrecognisable from the beginnings of my journey with Him by my side.

## Slingshot

*Psalm 27:10 NLT*
[10] Even if my father and mother abandon me, the LORD will hold me close.

*Psalm 68:5 NIV*
[5] A father to the fatherless, a defender of widows, is God in his holy dwelling.

*Psalm 34:18-19 ESV*
[18] The Lord is near to the broken hearted and saves the crushed in spirit. [19] Many are the afflictions of the righteous, but the Lord delivers him out of them all.

---

Reflection 26:

Have you ever been in such a dark hole you wanted to end the pain and torment?
What caused you to feel this way?
Was it abandonment, shame, rejection, loss, abuse?

Reflect upon your experiences that led you to such a place with a good counsellor. It's important to get help with this so you don't end up going back into that black hole, but see the light of fresh understanding and gain healing.

Do you know Jesus as your personal Saviour and Lord? Reflect upon this question before you read any further, and journal your thoughts, and if you do not yet know Jesus Christ in a personal way, now is your time!

---

# Day 27: Challenge and a way forward

You might be thinking you're reading this by accident, but with God there are no such accidents because He already knew you would have this little book in your hands.

You were called and led to read this book right now, or you wouldn't be reading it even if you found it, or were given it. I believe it is a God designed plan of His that you're here now reading this.

If you feel you want to know Jesus in a personal way, to receive Him into your life as your Lord and Saviour here is a simple prayer of repentance.

Dear Lord Jesus, I know I am a sinner and have done wrong things.
I believe You died for my sins, and you are the forgiver of my sins.
Right now, I turn from my sins and open the door of my heart, and my life.
I say sorry to you Lord with all my heart.
Please come and take and use my life, Lord. I've made such a mess of my life. Please come and straighten my life out.
I confess You as my personal Lord and Savior. Amen.

Your next step is to join a well-balanced non-toxic church. What do I mean by a non-toxic church? A church that teaches sound biblical doctrine, not manmade rules and control over you.

Jesus died to set us free, He paid the price of our sin, to give to us the precious gift of eternal life in heaven by God the Father after our short life here on earth is over.
A life that is free of all pain and sickness.

God knows our heart motives and reads our thoughts; He sees everything we do. We cannot trick God or pull the wool over His eyes. We cannot fake repentance to God. He knows when we are genuinely repenting, and when we are not being really open and honest.

We all sin. The difference between a believer and a non-believer is that we become redeemed sinners as opposed to condemned sinners. Not one of us is perfect or better than anyone else. God is the only one who can judge us, not people. We are called to love people, not judge them. That's God's role.

We've all sinned, we will sin, because we are human not divine. God loves everyone, His biggest desire is for all people to turn and run into His loving open arms and respond to His calling us to Him. To respond to His Son Jesus Christ, seek forgiveness and repent of our wrong doings, and come into a new way of life and living. A better life than the one we have when we try to live life by ourselves shutting God out.

But it is up to us, it is our choice, and our decision. God never forces anyone! It is up to us to decide to choose His way or our way. God is the creator of all things. He created the universe and everything in it. He created us in our mother's womb. Not one of us is here by mistake, even if we were not planned to be here by human parents, however you came to be here on earth, know this!

God loves you! Yes you! He designed you; He created you to be you, you are wired the way you are in your brain because He wired you up to be who you are. And He has a plan for your life, a good plan if you let Him into your life as Lord and Saviour. This means following His way of living life not our way. And His way is always better and bigger than our way.

**Slingshot**

*Jeremiah 29:11-14 AMP*
[11] For I know the plans and thoughts that I have for you,' says the Lord, 'plans for peace and well-being and not for disaster, to give you a future and a hope. [12] Then you will call on Me and you will come and pray to Me, and I will hear [your voice] and I will listen to you. [13] Then [with a deep longing] you will seek Me and require Me [as a vital necessity] and [you will] find Me when you search for Me with all your heart. [14] I will be found by you,' says the Lord, 'and I will restore your fortunes and I will [free you and] gather you from all the nations and from all the places where I have driven you,' says the Lord, 'and I will bring you back to the place from where I sent you into exile.'

*Proverbs 3:5-6 NIV*
[5] Trust in the Lord with all your heart and lean not on your own understanding; 6 in all your ways submit to Him, and He will make your paths straight.

*2 Corinthians 12:10 ESV*
[10] For the sake of Christ, then, I am content with weaknesses, insults, hardships, persecutions, and calamities. For when I am weak, then I am strong.

*Isaiah 35:4 GNT*
[4] Tell everyone who is discouraged, Be strong and don't be afraid! God is coming to your rescue

*Philippians 4:13 AMP*
[13] I can do all things [which He has called me to do] through Him who strengthens and empowers me [to fulfil His purpose—I am self-sufficient in Christ's sufficiency; I am ready for anything and equal to

anything through Him who infuses me with inner strength and confident peace.

Reflection 27:

Have you ever felt exiled?
Have you ever felt lost and in a wilderness?

Reflect upon these times, how did you feel?

# Part 6

# Accepted just as we are

## Day 28: God takes us where we're at right where we are

Life does many things to us, good, bad, and all the shades of grey in between. Life experiences and childhood upbringing shape who we are, but God can take us as we are and change our lives for the better. I know because it's been my life story. God took me out of the gutter of life, and He has totally taken me and shaped me anew. It is a lifelong journey and every day is an adventure when you follow God's way and not our own.

Shame need not bar you, or anything you've done in your past. Shame lifts from us when we know Jesus as our Lord. Yes, it takes time to feel that difference in our daily lives and much healing, but, trust me, in time, we do change, grow, develop into new creatures with a far happier and better life. Trials and hard times still come along, but we have a friend in Jesus who steers and helps us and that is what sustains me during life's trials and hard times.

If you do respond and give your life to Jesus Christ, the next step besides finding a church family that feels right for you, is to also to decide to allow Jesus to be Lord of your life as well as the saviour of your life. This means obeying God's teaching in His Word, in his book of life. When we obey and implement how we are to live by following the example of how Jesus lived, we will start to live a better life.

Notice I said obey and implement.

We are no longer under the old agreement God had with His people in the Old Testament. Jesus died for us as the ultimate sacrifice for our sins. We no longer keep the old laws such as sacrificing for our sins, or not wearing mixed fibres. But we do keep the moral laws. These are to help us live a safer, happier, and healthier life. God knows the destruction adultery brings because it breaks up a family and causes so much pain to those concerned. So, the moral laws are a better way to live for all concerned.

Understanding the context of the day a scripture was written helps us to translate the meaning to our day in our time, and how we can implement and apply the truths to our lives.

The Old Testament allows us to see how people lived and the mistakes they made. The lessons we can learn teach us not to live our lives repeating the same mistakes. This will help us to implement the wisdom we can glean from the life stories we read about. Also, we can read about the good things people did, and learn from those too.

In the New Testament, Jesus is our master coach. He gave illustrations by telling stories called parables, to teach us important lessons about how we should live our lives. We can learn about the individual characters in the New Testament and see they too made mistakes, and this should inspire us because we want to develop and grow for ourselves.

We can avoid so much pain in our own lives if we learnt the lessons in God's Word, obeyed and applied His Word to our life, and implemented the lessons as we learn them.

The wisdom books, Ecclesiastes and Proverbs, can teach us so much about how to live a wise life. Information and knowledge are power, which gives us an upper hand in life to avoid so many rabbit holes and so many mistakes we can fall into and avoid such a lot of pain, heartache, and dangerous people.

## Slingshot

*Galatians 5:1 AMP*
[1] In [this] freedom Christ has made us free [and completely liberated us]; stand fast then, and do not be hampered and held ensnared and submit again to a yoke of slavery [which you have once put off].

*Proverbs 3:5–6 ESV*
[5] Trust in the LORD with all your heart,
and do not lean on your own understanding.
[6] In all your ways acknowledge him,
and he will make straight your paths.

*Proverbs 4:6-7 NLT*
[6] Don't turn your back on wisdom, for she will protect you.
Love her, and she will guard you.
[7] Getting wisdom is the wisest thing you can do!
And whatever else you do, develop good judgement.

*Proverbs 1:7 MSG*
[7] Start with God - the first step in learning is bowing down to God; only fools thumb their noses at such wisdom and learning.

---

Reflection 28:

Think about how you feel right now?
Is Jesus your friend, Saviour, and Lord?

Journal your thoughts and feelings.

---

When Jesus died painfully on the cross, He died to set us free from our past sinful life. We no longer need to carry that burden of shame that ensnared us into feeling enslaved and trapped in our past life. Yes, the consequences of our past might still be with us. For example, in my own life I committed adultery with a married man and became pregnant by this man who slowly and insidiously charmed his unsavoury lifestyle into my life, who told me he could not produce children so as not to worry about getting pregnant.

At first, he was all charm with a perfect crease in his suit trousers and a posh voice. My father said to me much later on after much pain and heartache, Wendy, he's one of those men who've had more women than you've had hot dinners. I carried that shame of my past very heavily, which did not help with comments made to me by some of my family. I truly felt that shame lift off me while I was on my knees in my tiny house on a cold kitchen floor confessing my sins and giving my life to Jesus Christ.

You too can feel the freedom and weight lifted off by the forgiveness of our Lord Jesus Christ. Salvation cannot be earned or bought. It is a free gift from Christ. All He asks in return is that we love Him and we see Him as our saviour, and our Lord; meaning we worship and serve Him alone, live by His example in God's word and follow His ways, and not those of the culture of our day.

## Day 29: A bad start does not mean a bad ending

We can all have a bad start in life. But Joyce Meyer demonstrates how God has used her life in amazing ways through her experience and testimony. She says that having a bad start does not mean we have to have a bad finish. The beginning is out of our control, but the finish, the end of our lives is up to us.

What will you choose?

Reflection 29:

I know it is unusual to have a reflection exercise this early in the day, but bear with me....

Reflect and journal your start in life - to where you are right now. Draw a life map from childhood to where you are currently in your life.

Think about where you would like to gain new growth, change your life, and where and how you would like to see your life finish.

I have personally reflected over and over about my childhood, my school days, which were a living hell for me. And my work life, and relationships.

I've had a lot of teaching and learning about how our childhood can shape us into the adults we become. I've had a lot of fresh new layers of understanding about myself. And thinking back to all I've done with my jobs and my experiences, it has helped me to see where I am now, and the things in life that give me my greatest joys were all the same things I loved doing and had fulfilled me growing up.

This reflection is especially important if you feel you are in the wilderness, lost, or stuck in a rut. Don't rush this. Spend time journalling all the good and the bad and all the shades in between because nothing is all good or all bad. You might see a new direction you can head towards, a completely fresh perspective or approach to doing things, or even learn why you react to certain things. Whatever you discover, I'm sure it will help you to grow yourself in some way.

New beginnings await us, which is for anyone willing to learn and grow and invest in ourselves to have a new beginning.

**Slingshot**

*2 Corinthians 5:17 NIV*
[17]Therefore, if anyone is in Christ, the new creation has come: The old has gone, the new is here!

Every day is a gift from God, a new beginning! Everyday!

# Day 30: Lack of direction

When we are not self-aware such as knowing who we are, why we are like we are, our personal emotional or memory triggers can easily upset us, causing us to be unaware if we're a safe person for others to be around.

And if we're not safe, why not? And how do we get the help we need? How do we know if we are an encouraging person to be with, or someone who is critical, condemning, a negative half empty person or a cup half full person, etc.?

A lack of self-awareness can affect our own lives and the lives of others, it can also stop us from developing our God-given potential.

The way we interact with other people is often affected by our experiences in life, the way we are wired, the way we were brought up, and how we've been treated in relationships. Cultural differences, even within the same country, can affect us and our thinking, behaviour, disappointments in life, rejections, betrayals, pain and heartache, and the company we keep. This list is not the full list by any means.

## Slingshot

*Galatians 5:22-23 ESV*
22 But the fruit of the Spirit is love, joy, peace, patience, kindness, goodness, faithfulness, 23 gentleness, self-control; against such things there is no law.

*Psalm 32:8 ESV*
8 I will instruct you and teach you in the way you should go;

I will counsel you with my eye upon you.

*Psalm 37:23-24 ESV*
[23] The steps of a man are established by the Lord,
when he delights in his way;
[24] though he fall, he shall not be cast headlong,
for the Lord upholds his hand.

---

Reflection 30:

Reflect and journal what triggers easily upset you?
We all have triggers, list on a scale of 1-10 your biggest to your lowest triggers.
1 = Low and 10 = high.

Think about these triggers and reflect on why you have graded them in the order you have.

---

# Day 31: Triggers and blind spots

One really good resource book that illustrates how we can affect our own life advancement or why we're not successful in sales, or managing how we interact with others is by Dale Carnegie, called *How to Win Friends and Influence People.*

If you're a sensitive person, or a person who can be triggered and react easily, it is a good idea to learn about emotional intelligence. Go get the tools you need to grow. This could be getting books on the subject, watching YouTube videos, finding a coach or mentor, or going to counselling to help you grow in fresh understanding of your triggers and why you react to them.

We can all grow in emotional intelligence and improve on this the rest of our lives. It is a well-known fact that our brains stop growing at the pace they did from childhood to adulthood. You can find results backing this from lots of different credible sources. Emotional intelligence, on the other hand, is something we have unlimited potential to continue growing in, so why not embrace the new you that can emerge from new information.

Knowing our tiggers is the first key to managing our triggers. If we live in denial of our triggers, and our blind spots, then we will never overcome the difficult situations we can find ourselves in throughout our lives.

If you are not a book reader, then listen to audiobooks on Audible or watch YouTube teaching on this subject.

Learn to respond - not react!

## Slingshot

*Philippians 4:13 AMP*
[13] I can do all things [which He has called me to do] through Him who strengthens *and* empowers me [to fulfil His purpose—I am self-sufficient in Christ's sufficiency; I am ready for anything and equal to anything through Him who infuses me with inner strength and confident peace.]

Reflection 31:

This reflection is one where you get brave, jump in, and only ask those who are mature and trustworthy, a person who knows you well. Don't ask an ultra-critical person, but a person who will give you sound truth. You need around three people IF you know this many people you can trust.

Ask them to tell you your blind spots, those things that none of us see about us for ourselves. Be gracious and not over-sensitive. Do not react. Go and quietly reflect upon their answers. Ask the Holy Spirit to talk to you about their answers.

Every time you are triggered into reacting to a situation, reflect on what it was that caused you to be triggered.

Was it a particular word, tone of voice, body language of another person, a particular setting, or event?

Do you feel the person you asked for feedback is right?
If so, what are you going to do differently now?

This takes a lot of practice to re-train our brains to act, talk, and think in a new way. I once heard it said it can take up to 66 days for our brains to be rewired and old patterns replaced.

So don't be hard on yourself, beat yourself up, or feel you've failed. NO, you have not failed. You've had an attempt, now it's time to retire that thought, replace, and restart.

Remember these 3 R's - Retire - Replace - Restart. (Dale Carnegie)

But never give up!

# Day 32: Who is in control?

Are you allowing others to control you? Or make your choices for you, and therefore allowing others to remove your right to have a voice in your life?

We can all find ourselves in damaging and controlling relationships from abusive control, emotional control, physical control, sexual control, mental control, or even abusive relationships in our childhood. These can be at school or home. As young adults onwards in the workplace, or been bullied in life and let down by those we trusted. All these situations can affect how we interact with others.

For children, the world of adults is very often a confusing place to understand without added issues to deal with while navigating their way through life as they grow up.

In my world as a child growing up, I was taught certain people in responsible roles in society were 'always' safe. I discovered the hard and painful way that they were not always safe people!

I thought that church going people were 'always' going to be safe people. But the sad reality is this is not the truth. Church is for damaged and imperfect people, and also for those who are whole and safe people to be with. So, we should not always assume 'everyone' who goes to church is a safe person, or every person in authority is a safe person, and this is true about any situation in life.

Be it our school, our neighbours, our work place, or our family, our safety in any situation we are in is dependent upon the people who teach us. The people who we live with, or we are surrounded by, work with, bosses, police, people in high positions in life, anywhere, at any time we could find ourselves in a situation that's not safe or healthy to be in, and that's the raw reality of life.

Learning about self-awareness is so important to know how to deal with and cope with certain situations. Who we are, and why we are who we are, is especially important for anyone in a leadership role, or, in a role of responsibility for the safety of others, whether children or vulnerable adults.

Having emotional intelligence is a crucial aspect of creating this safety because when we are aware of our emotions, we will know what causes our triggers to kick into action, which helps us to navigate all aspects of the world we live in. Who we hang out with and where we go, who we allow into our inner circle, the people we listen to, the roles we have in life and how we manage our relationships all shape the world we live in.

Knowing and understanding ourselves will help us to make wise decisions about the people we spend time with and who we listen to in order to recognise what triggers our emotional responses. We can learn to both recognise when and how we've been provoked and then be able to take better charge of our emotional responses and reactions.

To stay safe in an often-unsafe world, we must set proper boundaries to keep ourselves on the right track. We want to be able to stay safe and stop ourselves from going down a rabbit hole out of our emotional needs not being met, which could lead to much misery, pain and heartache. However, we slowly discover we've gone along a path that leads us to trust and give our intimate self to the wrong person, and thereby get entangled in dangerous, damaging, controlling and abusive relationships.

To jump to a sidenote here, a friend introduced me to a book called *Boundaries* by Dr. Henry Cloud and Dr. John Townsend. This book helped me learn how to set and keep safe boundaries. It took a lot of practice, determination, and constant effort not to fall into the usual rabbit holes. I've failed from time to time, but every time I learn new knowledge about myself, and how I could avoid falling down yet another rabbit hole. Now I find it's much easier to stop repeating the same mistakes.

I know from personal experiences what I am talking about after going through two damaging broken marriages, damaging controlling relationships, sexual abuse, physical abuse, domestic abuse, emotional abuse, and psychological abuse. These traps, my rabbit holes, were my bad choices in life, my mistakes, and my lack of wisdom. The root cause I discovered by receiving the teaching and counselling was not feeling valued by family, school teachers, peers, so-called childhood friends, and work situations. The desperate need to feel wanted, valued, loved, accepted, or worthy had led me into so much pain, confusion and damage. It's taken me years and years to fully recover. And quite a lot of counselling. My need for others' approval, caused by my unmet childhood needs, left me feeling unvalued, and without a voice. I can see looking back this created a lot of painful learning about life, that at times almost finished me off, crippled me and caused even more damaging results.

I've been a single mother, desperate and in yet another damaging and controlling relationship that took me years to realise and understand why I repeated my mistakes. I've come to acknowledge that abusive and controlling people have different faces, shapes, sizes, backgrounds, and jobs. They use various forms of abuse to control, hurt, and fulfil their own needs to make them feel in the power seat and not me. Or to punish me for some stuff that happened to them in life, a type of revenge for the pain that they suffered, and they saw me as an easy victim. My abusers disempowered me and made me feel smaller than I am (inwardly speaking and in terms of mindset damage); therefore, I never saw the abuse as abuse. Instead, the abuse made me feel stupid, all wrong about myself, lacking confidence, beat me down into compliance, shame, dirty, inadequate, thick, ridiculous, and fear of all kinds, one being that I would never ever be wanted by anyone else because I wasn't good enough and so on.

A lot of people are hurting and lonely and are forced to hide the hurt and abuse behind closed doors! I am praying that this book will somehow in some way reach out to those who suffer behind closed doors too. And in some way help to release them, empower them to see the truth of who they are, and they will reach out for support and receive safe help, and ultimately freedom to be themselves, and live their life as God intended, free, and not under the control of others.

## Slingshot

*Proverbs 27:17 AMP*
[17] As iron sharpens iron,
So one man (or woman) sharpens [and influences] another [through discussion].

In other words, a good relationship makes you a better person. A friend who sharpens you helps you fulfil your God-given purpose. Look for friends who will speak truth in love to you. Their constructive criticism can boost your spiritual growth. But only ask trusted people you know well and will tell you the truth in love, and those who will not break your confidences you've shared with them.

Healthy relationships are not all giving or all taking. A healthy relationship is of mutual benefit to both people. Dr. Dharius Daniels' book *Relational Intelligence* explains very well about how to understand relationships and get our relationships into the right categories.

Laquonne Holden's book *Relationshift* is also a good book about relationships.
Note from Joyce Meyer's *Study Bible* on page 2063 in James Chapter 5- Tell the right person.

Anything we feel we have to hide has power over us, but when things are exposed, the truth will make us free. Be spirit-led. Choose someone you know you can trust, someone who is understanding and will not judge you.

Using wisdom and balance is so important in these matters. If you are going to share your problems with someone, let God show you who to choose as a confidant. Pick a mature believer, someone who will not be burdened or harmed by what you share or use it to hurt you or make you feel worse about yourself.

*Proverbs 17:17 AMP*
[7] A friend loves at all times,
And a brother is born for adversity.

What is Soloman saying in that verse? He is pointing out that a true friend and a true brother (or sister in Christ) is always loving and helps us in trying times. A true friend, a true brother or sister in Christ whose friendship is genuine will always show true love to us even in bad or low times, or our worse circumstances, even when others turn against us, or we lose everything we own, as well as the happy good times.

*Proverbs 4:23 AMP*
[23] Watch over your heart with all diligence,
For from it *flow* the springs of life.

When someone injures us, if someone is not a safe person for us to be around, God says forgive them their sins against us. But we must watch over and protect our hearts. Because out of our heart flows life! This is why it's so important we get our relationships right.

We must learn to navigate the relationships we have in our life because God wants you to protect your heart.

---

Reflection 32:

Reflect and journal about the types of hurt and pain you've had in your life.

It might be a very short list, or a very long one, but getting it out and writing it on paper helps you to begin that journey of letting go of what you've buried for so long.

If you need further help and counselling for anything that has surfaced, do not bury it once again, find help to talk it through with a good counsellor. Talk to your doctor for advice. They may well help you to get the right counsellor for your needs.

The personal growth program I joined, led by Dr. Dharius Daniels, and the teaching given has had an immense effect upon me. I now see who I am, why I am who I am, and I've had a lot of deep healing through fresh understanding of myself. I'm a totally different person, much calmer, steady emotionally, no longer uprooted, or allowing what others say to me by the names they try to land on me, upset or confuse me, or affect

---

me the same as they used to. After eighteen months, Wow! What a transformation!

The transformational coaching program for personal growth I belong to is danielsden.com
Check it out. It's a place where we support, encourage, love and value each other.
Lifelong learning for those who want to grow till they go!

# Day 33: Me finding me, might help you find you

Learning who I am in Jesus Christ and that he loved me, and would have died for me on that cross, even if I was the only person alive on earth, was massive to me. It took me years to really unpack the power of fully embracing this truth, even after I had given my life to Christ. To understand that God accepts me as I am, just as I am, was immense after all the abuse and loneliness I had suffered. I can only tell you about my experience, because none of us can give our felt experiences to others, we can only talk and share about what happened.

About two years ago, I read the best book I've ever read on relational intelligence, by Dr. Dharius Daniels. A brilliant practical book, so well written. It revolutionised the way I see relationships, and how I've called a person a friend far too fast, way before they've earned that privilege to be called a friend.

Pastor Laqounne Holden also has a good book on relationships called *Relationshift*. This is worded slightly differently, but the principles are exactly the same.

Not knowing ourselves and why we do what we do, enables others to have the power seat of our emotions and control us through our emotions without us being aware and realising this.
Joyce Meyer has a very clever and easy way to think about life here. Her catchy saying has stuck by me ever since.

 "Who is driving your bus, you, or others?"

She said that buses pick people up, and let people off the bus during its journey along its route. And in life, some people get on our bus, and as we move through our life journey, others get off our bus. But, "we" should be in charge of our own bus, and decide who gets on and off our bus. Ever since I heard this, I've asked myself the question, "Am I driving my own bus? Or others driving me?" I spend every few months evaluating this question.

Dr. Dharius Daniels puts this analogy as the gate we need to be in control of, who are we allowing in our gate, and who do we need to let out of our gate? Different seasons bring different reasons people become part of our lives. And seasons vary in length of time, that's why evaluating our relationships is important. Who we spend our time with can help or hinder our wellbeing, our personal growth, our mindset, our happiness, our peace, our joy, and even our health.

Sometimes we struggle for various reasons to let go of those who we need to let go of, or who want to leave and we make it hard for them to leave. I've heard several well trusted, well renowned preachers say that if people want to leave, let them leave! If people do not want to be in our lives, then just maybe, they're not meant to be in our lives, so let them go!

Seasons can vary in terms of the length of time, or reason people are in our lives. Bishop Jakes once said, "If you've got one good solid friend in your life, then you're blessed." So, if we've got more than one, or a friend that sticks with us in the good and the bad, the smooth and the rough seasons of our lives, then we're really blessed.

**Slingshot**

*Proverbs 18:24 ESV*
[24] A man of many companions may come to ruin,
but there is a friend who sticks closer than a brother.

*Ecclesiastes 7:8-9 ESV*
[8] Better is the end of a thing than its beginning,
and the patient in spirit is better than the proud in spirit.
[9] Be not quick in your spirit to become angry,
for anger lodges in the heart of fools.

*2 Peter 1:5-7 NIV*
[5] For this very reason, make every effort to add to your faith goodness;
and to goodness, knowledge; [6] and to knowledge, self-control; and to
self-control, perseverance; and to perseverance, godliness; [7] and to
godliness, mutual affection; and to mutual affection, love.

Healthy relationships are mutually beneficial. If we are doing all the
giving, and the other persons doing all the taking, then it's not mutually
beneficial. Or if the other person is doing all the giving and we're the
one doing all the taking, it's not a healthy relationship.

---

Reflection 33:

Who is driving your bus?
Who are you allowing to drive your bus? Who are you letting in through
your gate?
Who needs to get off your bus? Who needs to get out of your gate?
Are you trying to hold onto people, relationships, a particular job, a
situation, even a church you need to let go of?

Ask yourself, why are you allowing others to be in the driving seat of
your bus or in your gate?

Reflect and Journal on these questions.

---

# Part 7

# Assessment time!

# Day 34: Buses, gates and boundaries

Only by spending some time assessing our relationships can we understand who should be on our bus or who should get off our bus. Only by reflection can we see who needs to be let in to our gate, and who needs to go out of our gate.

Dr. Dharius Daniels teaches in his book *Relational Intelligence*, how to categorise our relationships to see who fits into what category. This is important because it helps us to understand where we should give our precious time to, how much, and where we need to be giving more of our time. We can tell ourselves that we're spending more time with our spouse and family than we actually are in reality.

It helps us to realign our lives and refocus our attention where we need to. We can see if we're wasting our time instead of investing it to advance us further towards our dream and our purpose. Are we spending time with people who don't understand our needs and interests? Have these people changed? We can change in terms of not wanting to drink copious amounts of alcohol, and the friends we used to hang out with still want that lifestyle.

We cannot move into the new that God has for us to step into, unless we can let go of the old that's holding us back. Whether it's out of insecurity or fear, only we can decide enough is enough. As Joyce Meyer teaches, we will put up with what we tolerate. When we've reached the point of enough is enough, and our limit of what we will tolerate changes, we can understand things need to change in order for us to reach our vision, or our new goal and the next level.

This should be the point where we get brave and say, "We need a frank conversation."

This is if we know a frank conversation is the safe option. For me, it wasn't the safe option in two particular relationships. I had to take steps to protect myself, my baby and my toddler without letting my unsafe husband realise. I had to be wise!

The situation, the circumstances, and the person involved should all be taken into careful consideration before you have an open conversation. Sometimes you can decide to recategorise a relationship and not say anything to the person concerned. It can be enough that you know you've decided to not be as open, but share as much, give as much of yourself, see them as much as you want to.

My coach teaches us to be prepared for anything after the conversation. Because we are in control of ourselves and how we speak, what we say, and our body language, we can get it all right yet it still goes all wrong. Because we will never be in control of anyone else or their reaction, no matter how well we did, we are never going to know the other person's reaction.

So be prepared for negative or emotional outbursts, or anger, and decide before you have the conversation how you will react to any unexpected outburst.

---

Reflection 34:

After the previous reflection, did you manage to let go of the people you needed to let off your bus and out your gate?

How do you feel after mentally letting them go?
Do you also need to physically set new boundaries?
How are you going to achieve this, and keep your boundaries set?

---

You need to create a strategy you can work to, your plan of action.

Even do nothing until you've invested in yourself and read the *Relational Intelligence* book by Dr. Dharius Daniels, and Dr. Henry Cloud's book *Boundaries*.

Emotional Boundaries, relational boundaries and mindset boundaries, are all important and can keep us safe and mentally healthy. This won't come overnight, and you might need a person to help you, support you, and encourage you to continue to hold your new mindset about the boundaries you've set.

Do you need to pray about this and ask God's Holy Spirit to guide you, give you the wisdom and the strength to achieve this?
Look up Dr. Henry Cloud's YouTube teaching sessions on the topic of safe people and how to spot unsafe people.

Buy Dr. Henry Cloud's books on: *Boundaries, Safe People, and Necessary Endings*.

And I am so grateful now I look back with eyes that can understand just how awesome God is, and how He protected me by removing me out of those very unsafe relationships, even before I knew him personally, and I didn't need to do anything. At the time, it was a very devastating situation. I was totally rocked to the point of suicide; I thought the world had ended. I wish that I had the gift of information and the knowledge back then that I've got now. That's why I decided to write this little book. By sharing my life and all I've learnt I'm hoping to help you!

## Day 35: Step into the new - out of the old

Now, I praise and thank God for His timely interventions in my life. And through those experiences I've learnt to never hang onto anyone who wants to walk out of my life. I just let them go, and I never chase after anyone who decides to walk out of my life including family at one point. Yes, that hurt, it hurt really bad, deeply, the shock almost put me under, but I came through it a much stronger better person, and I no longer need anyone's approval to live my life, including family.

Reflect upon your relationships, how healthy are they for you?
Do you need to let go of some relationships?
Do your relationships build you, encourage you, and support you?
Or do they devalue you, make you feel smaller than you are, intimidate you? Are they controlling? Tearing you down, are you fearful to be around them?

As we grow, we can suddenly find ourselves having outgrown people and having nothing in common any more. It does not mean we let go of all our relationships, because we don't ever want to get to a place of looking down on other people either. We're no better than other people and we need to remember that. The relationships that stop us growing, or those that are damaging to us are the ones we let go of, abusive or controlling relationships either physically, emotionally, or sexually, those that mentally prevent us seeing the real us, or cause us to see ourselves less than God created us to be.

**Slingshot**

*Psalm 139:14-15 ESV*
[14] I praise you, for I am fearfully and wonderfully made.
Wonderful are your works;

my soul knows it very well.

[15] My frame was not hidden from you,

when I was being made in secret,

intricately woven in the depths of the earth.

---

Reflection 35:

Reflect on how you see yourself. What would your new self look like, and what old things do you need to leave behind to press forwards?

---

# Day 36: Flying free

This can be your life too. You can be set free too. My first step was to give my life to Christ, and trust in God to provide for me, and let go of the chains that were dragging me back down the same old rabbit holes. It was hard. It took a long time, forty years, and it took much practice, but finally I've arrived. And, so can you. Where are you on your journey to discovering who you are, and what your potential is that has been hidden deep inside, that even you don't know that God put within you when He created you in your mother's womb? Time to start discovering just who you really are, and what your God given potential is and can be unlocked, and, as I have discovered it's never too late in life to begin that journey.

I watched Bishop Jake give a sermon a long time ago called *Chain Breaker*.

It really made sense to me why I kept going back to the same negative situations, what was the reason I could not seem to break free.

Bishop Jakes had a dog called Pup. He was a strong dog and because where they lived was near to a road, and Pup liked to chase any passing traffic, the dog was on a chain to prevent him running off. One day the chain broke and the dog ran after the passing car. I think this was the story, but the part I remembered most was about gravity.

Bishop Jakes talked about gravity pulling us back. He said when an aeroplane takes off the runway, it has to break free of the gravity pull. That's like us, we try to take off, to get free, but gravity pulls us back, like the chain pulled Pup back.

Once the aeroplane has broken free of that gravity pull, it can be free to fly. And we need to get past that gravity pull to fly higher and be free to fly. Or to break free from the chains that are holding us back like they did Pup, in order to break free from that old behaviour.

That picture helped me immensely. I understood it was the old pulling me back, the old patterns, the old conditioning, the old mindset, and the false obligations put on me I felt I had to keep. The compliant child was still saying yes, you've got to obey, but who was I obeying and why?

## Slingshot

*Isaiah 40:31 ESV*
[31] but they who wait for the Lord shall renew their strength;
they shall mount up with wings like eagles;
they shall run and not be weary;
they shall walk and not faint.

---

Reflection 36:

Reflect upon any repeated negative patterns and ask yourself are you being pulled back by gravity?

What do you need to reframe about any thoughts that create those negative patterns?
Where did they originate from?
How can you move forward into your new self to allow you to fly free?

Where are you on your journey to be authentically you?
Journal your thoughts.

---

# Day 37: Burn out

There are all sorts of reasons we find ourselves being over-busy and overstretched. It comes from being unable to say no, the job pressures, the deadlines, the financial pressures, being unable to set safe boundaries, being a single parent, and needing others' approval, to name a few.

We moved to Wesley Theological College for my husband to train for the Methodist ministry. At that time, we had four children and no savings, still owing money on our tiny house before it sold. Life was tough. We were given a set amount to live on for seventeen weeks at a time. We were lucky enough to be granted accommodation within the college, in the principal's house after the principal and his lovely wife moved into a purpose-built bungalow on the college grounds. From what I remember, we were given just over £2,000 for the seventeen weeks, but around £1,000 of that money had to be used for heating costs and electricity, etc. With four growing children, two teen girls, our energetic son who suddenly had the safe space to charge around on his bike, and our youngest daughter, the money didn't even cover food, never mind school uniform, school trips, shoes and coats. Therefore, I went to work to support my husband in his training and our family.

I started to do some cleaning jobs because that was the only work available to me. However, this involved travel. We took the decision to let our car go because we couldn't afford to keep it, so now there were bus fares to find for myself and the older girls.

I cleaned for very nice people who lived in beautiful big houses, and an apartment in select areas of Bristol. From memory, in two of these places, there were sixty-two steps from bottom to top, as the stairs curled round from the bottom to the top of these three storey houses. There were several bathrooms, and lots of beautiful or valuable things to clean and care for. One family I used to clean for had always employed an au pair before, but they decided instead to employ a cleaner to come and clean everywhere in one day. This house also had a granny flat (annexe) at the top with a bathroom and kitchenette, which their teenage daughter occupied.

I would work for them eight to eight and a half hours in one day. Collect all the dirty washing, do all the laundry and ironing, put all the ironing away, clean from the top to the bottom of the house including all bedrooms, strip the beds, clean all bathrooms, the massive kitchen, and laundry room. The white floor in the kitchen, the drying room and the laundry area took me one and a half hours to clean alone, especially with the family's two cats who came and went as they pleased bringing with them dirt on the nice clean floor, there were two cookers to clean, and clean the windows.

This was after getting up really early, getting my children organised, doing the pots, taking the youngest two to school, walking to the bus stop, waiting for the bus, getting off at Clifton shops, walking another twenty minutes to start the cleaning, walking back twenty minutes to Clifton shops, buying food, waiting for a bus which sometimes took me an hour before one would stop with enough space to get on board. Then I had to walk down the long road back to college. Once home there was a meal for six people to prepare while at the same time trying to listen to and minister to all my kids' woes of the day. Then it was time to get the little ones to bed, prepare the packed lunches for the next day, clean shoes, sort washing, and pots, and fall into bed.

My reputation of being a hard worker, who was trustworthy, reliable, capable and able to be left to get on with it, and being trusted with a key, meant I was offered more work. I coped very well for a long time, and ended up cleaning for five people. But as the time went on, and the lugging of heavy food after a long day cleaning, going home to tackle meals and all my own cleaning and managing four children who had various needs, all at different stages of need and development, and listening to my husband and supporting him began to take its toll.

I ended up with burn out, which took me over eighteen months to recover from. I vowed and declared after that lesson I would never again take on too much of anything not ever again, and I have not.

It's so easy to add task after task, and feel flattered to be asked to do or join one thing after another. We all like to feel wanted, or that we can be super men and women, or take on the promotion at work, or add roles people want us to do, or be a part of a committee and so on. I found I was coping really well and then all of a sudden, I hit a brick wall of overload. It's great when the kids are well, when we are well, and all things are swimming along nicely, but life happens to all of us. The unexpected comes to hit all of us out of the blue, it's these times we find that our overload has left us no flexibility to breathe.

Sometimes, we need time to breathe, reflect, and be rather than to do. As Christians, we know we have an enemy who does not want us to have a fulfilling life of abundant joy, the life Jesus Christ wants us to have and died for us to have. Satan wants us to fall down that rabbit hole of doing too much. He knows if he can get us so tired that we do not have the time to think and reflect to hear God's voice, that he can start to play his mind games. We cannot hear the voice of God speaking to us if we are so exhausted and so busy with meeting schedules that we do not set aside time every day to be with God, in quiet, to hear what He wants to tell us, instruct us to do or say.

Reflection 37:

Have you ever been too busy to have that quiet time with God and hear God's voice?

Have you ever experienced burnout, or overload?

If so, how did this impact you and your life?

Journal your reflection.

## Day 38: Time and space

Give yourself the love of time and space to sit quietly with God to hear His Voice.

The arrow of time goes one way!
From our birth to our death.

I heard Joyce Meyer say time is the one thing we can never get a refund on! And that hit me hard.

Time is our most precious commodity and we should never take the time we have for granted.

I also heard it said that the average lifespan of a person is 72.5 years. So, if we take our age away from this, it gives us an idea of how many summers we have left to live. Obviously, this isn't set in stone, and there's lots of variables. If we're lucky we live way beyond 72 years of age. I certainly hope I do. But it made me sit up straight! I was 67 years old then. Wow! That's five summers I have left to make a difference, live a better life, and create an impact that enhances other people's lives. It sure gave me focus!

My days never go as well if I try to handle them without the wisdom, help and guidance throughout my day, which only God can give me.

If you're a busy mum as I was years ago, even a few moments alone to ask for the help and guidance you need for that day will make a dramatic difference to your day.

I used to pray as I worked, cleaning, washing the pots, walking to work, and cleaning for people. I found even just five minutes alone with God made a huge impact on my day. Today, we can watch online teachings on YouTube or listen to books by these great preachers on Audible as we work, walk, or exercise.

A quick help to me was a small book of the promises God made to us written in His word, and Joyce Meyer's little book of power words taken from the Bible. I followed a daily reading online, by post, or by an email subscription from a good and solid doctrinal teacher.

Elevation Church's Pastor Steven Furtick has a one minute a day reflection.

Joyce Meyer also has email subscriptions for her different online teachings.

Pastor Rick Warren has his daily devotional readings.

My pastor, Dr. Dharius Daniels of Change Church has many YouTube teachings you can dip in and out of, as do those I've already mentioned.

I've listed some of the inspiring preachers who have helped me deepen my understanding of God's Word, helped me to grow, and also challenged me in varying ways. (You can find their website addresses at the back of this book)

Dr. Dharius Daniels, Change Church.
Bishop T.D. Jakes, Potters House Church.
Pastor Keion Henderson, Lighthouse Church.
Pastor Stephen Furtick, Elevation Church.
Dr. Charles Stanley, In Touch Ministries.
Joyce Meyer

Christine Caine, you can find on YouTube, she is a well-known speaker, and author.
Sarah Jakes-Roberts, and Cora Jakes-Coalman, also at Potters House Church.
Priscilla Shirer, Going Beyond Ministries.
Tony Evans
Pastor Rick Warren

These are a few great faithful teachers of God's word I have watched and listened to for quite a few years. I pray every morning to know God's ways, for His wisdom which far surpasses human wisdom, and for His help to meet the challenges of the day to come.

Give yourself some self-love, time and space for God to speak to you. Ask Him for guidance on what to drop out of if you've fallen into the rabbit hole of being too busy. Start a new plan of action that considers spending just a few minutes with God, who loves you so much. This time will help you meet the day's challenges with His grace and His wisdom. Five minutes with Him in prayer and quiet, honouring Him as you get out of bed to start your day, and asking Him for help in all you do, will make a massive difference to your days and your life.

**Slingshot**

*Romans 10:17 ESV*
[17] So faith comes from hearing, and hearing through the word of Christ.

*Jeremiah 33:3 ESV*
[3] Call to me and I will answer you, and will tell you great and hidden things that you have not known.

God's word tells us that in order to hear the secret things of God hidden in the scriptures, we need to know Him, and the way to know God is through His Son Jesus Christ.

*John 14:6 ESV*
[6] Jesus said to him, "I am the way, and the truth, and the life. No one comes to the Father except through me."

*Hebrews 2:1 ESV*
[1] Therefore we must pay much closer attention to what we have heard, lest we drift away from it.

*John 8:47 ESV*
[47] Whoever is of God hears the words of God. The reason why you do not hear them is that you are not of God."

*John 16:13 ESV*
[13] When the Spirit of truth comes, he will guide you into all the truth, for he will not speak on his own authority, but whatever he hears he will speak, and he will declare to you the things that are to come.

---

Reflection 38:

When was the last time you sat in silence to hear from God?
How can you love yourself more?
Have you heard God speak to you lately?
How can you find that space to hear from God?
If you feel too busy, where can you create that few moments of space for you?

---

# Day 39: With God I can!

The key to inner growth is being open to hear what God is saying to us. How do we do this?

God tells us in His Word, that we need a daily transforming of our mind. This only comes from studying the Word of God daily. This does not need to be a long-winded study, or necessarily lots of reading. It could be one verse that speaks to us, or studying on a particular subject or theme.

We can fall into the trap of thinking that reading a lot is better, but reading just for the sake of reading is meaningless because it doesn't feed us spiritually, that means it doesn't benefit us as much as it could. We need to approach reading in ways that would nourish us. We could simply read so we can tick off the box on our calendar to say we've done the reading for that day enabling us to achieve reading the bible in a year. There is nothing wrong with this if it feeds and inspires us, and we've taken the time and effort to unpack what we've read of God's Word we've put the time and effort into.

This mindset can sometimes be a trap of the enemy to make us believe we've achieved our spiritual growth goal. Conversely, it can be an attack of the enemy if we fail to meet our self-imposed reading schedule and start to feel we've let God down by not achieving our own goal. Don't be a slave to catching up out of false guilt if you miss a day's reading you've set as your target. Bible study is not meant to become a chore.

Reading is one thing, but reading to be fed spiritually and grow is another thing altogether. When we read to grow, we need to understand what we've read, the literal meaning and what it means for us. Dr. Dharius Daniels teaches something called, 'squeeze the word.'

For years and years this is how I learnt to grow spiritually. I learnt this through the pattern of Community Bible Study International. I took it for granted that all believers had this same or similar pattern of learning, and this is how every new convert to Christ learnt. I learnt God's Word for thirteen and half years in this way, which truly was a gift from God, and my pathway to learning and spiritual growth. At the time I had no idea how huge a privilege this was because I assumed it was the norm and that everyone did this.

What a blessing and what a privilege it was to be a part of such a new movement in Christian learning in the UK. After leaving Bolsover Methodist Church in Derbyshire for my husband to train for the ministry, I soon discovered this was not the case. I felt bereft of the friends I had been used to being there, my husband's family, all I had known for years where I was loved and accepted for who I am by the wonderful people who brought me to Christ, and my support network.

**Slingshot**

*Philippians 4:13 AMP*
[13] I can do all things [which He has called me to do] through Him who strengthens *and* empowers me [to fulfil His purpose—I am self-sufficient in Christ's sufficiency; I am ready for anything and equal to anything through Him who infuses me with inner strength and confident peace.]

I have grown immensely since belonging to Change Church and being under Dr. Dharius Daniels' teaching ministry, especially as I poured more and more time into learning during COVID-19. I have learnt so much. During Dr. Daniels' teaching, I learnt how he squeezes the Word. He has now started bibleu.academy which is invaluable for anyone wanting to learn more about the bible. I realised I had been doing this all my Christian life since I gave my life to serve Christ. This realisation was so exciting for me.

It affirmed me and helped me to realise I might be dyslexic and have no qualifications, but that means nothing! I was learning far faster and having great leaps of spiritual growth than I had ever had. I always told myself I could not study like others do because I could not read or write as people were supposed to until I was eleven.

When I was around thirty-two years old, I discovered I was also dyslexic. I said to myself, oh well then, you cannot do or understand like others with academic ability and that's that. I now realise how wrong I have been to believe that. I have much to offer to others. I can share my experiences to nurture others, like myself, who have never had the good fortune to feel anyone was ever interested in themselves or believed in them.

If this is you as well, then LISTEN! God can teach us more through His Word than any other book about life and how to live a successful life. Because He created us in our mother's womb, He formed us, He has a plan for our life, and a good plan, His Word says so. He knows what is in us because He put it there and can and will pull out of us what He put into us at the right time, in His perfect timing.

Don't beat yourself up anymore saying I cannot, instead say "with God's help I can!"

Reflection 39:

Where are you right now in your walk with God?
Close, distant, feeling like He doesn't care for you?

Reflect upon your thoughts, and journal them.

Be honest. God knows anyway, so you might as well be honest.
If you feel distant, ask God's Holy Spirit to come and help you. It may
not happen in an instant, but keep praising and thanking Him that He
cares about you, loves you, and your sudden moment of feeling closer
to God will come.

# Day 40: Squeeze the word!

Squeeze the Word. And here is how.

If you're not sure where to begin, start with Proverbs, the wisdom book for how to live a safe and wise life. Or one of the gospels in the New Testament. Read a few verses of a Proverb, or from your chosen book in the New Testament. What is it saying literally?

Then study to see what the context is, use a google search or bible commentaries. Then read it again, and see if any of the words jump out at you. Something may jump out, or maybe nothing that time.

Write out or circle the words that stand out that you feel are speaking personally to you. God can communicate with us in this way. For me, there were so many times this approach has shown me what direction God is leading me in for that moment, situation, or season, or a word of wisdom about a subject, situation, or relationship I needed knowledge about. Sometimes God uses this to speak to me about future events that would take place in my life, so I hang onto these and write them down, knowing that in God's perfect timing, these will come to pass. Sometimes it can help me see the part I need to do before God then comes and does the parts I cannot do. It's so I can choose to prepare myself, gain new skills or learn about something so I am ready when God brings to pass what He showed me.

I will follow any other references that may come up under the text I've just read and repeat the process. We can gain more insight this way to grow faster and deeper rather than simply reading large amounts each day or shutting our eyes and opening the bible and reading where our finger lands. This approach is very hit-and-miss. We can read something way out of context and go down the wrong rabbit holes. Or we can behave in a totally unwise way and get completely off track. We are wasting our precious time and causing ourselves much stress we didn't need to be adding to our lives.

Try squeezing the Word and see what happens. Just to say, God's Word is full of hidden meanings and messages God only reveals to those who have given their lives to him by repenting their sins and inviting Him in (see Day 27 for further explanation), His Word says this. Once we belong to Christ, God's Word opens up its hidden truths to believers. If you already belong to Christ, and have never tried this method, give it a go but hang onto your hat because you're in for an exciting ride!

A new beginning awaits those who seek! And walking in step with God, allowing Him to lead the way by His Holy Spirit guiding us, there's never a day when I have not learnt something new. I've had a much more exciting journey since I've walked within the rhythm of where the Holy Spirit has led me rather than walking by myself and trying to live how I think things should happen or be.


## Slingshot

*Psalm 1:2-3 AMP*
2 But his delight is in the law of the Lord,
And on His law [His precepts and teachings] he [habitually] meditates day and night.
3 And he will be like a tree *firmly* planted [and fed] by streams of water,
Which yields its fruit in its season;
Its leaf does not wither;
And in whatever he does, he prospers [and comes to maturity].

Reflection Exercise 40:

Start to discover deeper meaning in God's word by a new journey of squeezing the word.

Write out in your journal what verse you read, any words you've circled, and anything you feel God is saying to you.

Pray about what you feel God is saying to you, and think and meditate on the verse and the words for that day. If necessary for longer than that.

Journalling our progress makes it interesting to read later down the road. It'll be interesting to see our growth when we look back on our journey.

When we spend time in daily study of God's Word and meditate upon what He has told us, taught us, instructed us to do, and how to behave, we are being transformed bit by bit, slowly, incrementally growing, daily. Then we start to become more mature in our faith, and mature in our knowledge. And what we've learnt and the way we think, speak, and behave changes.

Slow incremental growth will lead to quantum leaps that lead us to a better life by living our life God's way.

It's never too late to grow, change, and live a better, more joyful life.

So, pack your suitcase and be ready for more new adventures. BUT before you go, a few words from less vulnerable me to less vulnerable you:

I pray you've had some mindset shifts and you are starting a new journey to a new you! And seek out further help finding you if you need this next step.

I am praying for your new journey to finding a new version of you continues.

I am praying that you've been blessed by taking the time for you, to reflect and know yourself better.

I am praying that you're set free to be who God created you to be.

I am praying you're out of your cage and flying high above any new storms like an eagle does.

(Eagles deliberately fly towards a storm and rise up to fly above it, and from the quiet peace above the storm, they look down at the storm for a place of calm.)

I am praying you see yourself as God sees you, beautifully made.

I am praying your life is spiritually richer and you continue to grow in God's Word and His ways, and His wisdoms.

As Joyce Meyer once said:
Wisdom does now what wisdom will be happy with later,

Carnality (our feelings and emotions) does what feels good now and pays later,
And later always comes!

I am praying you live a happier and wiser life for the journey you've begun, and every day is a new adventure in your progress.

Thank you for taking this journey with me. I've enjoyed your company. May God bless you and keep you, send His Angels to minister to you, and surround you with His love, Amen.

# Further recommended reading

**Books:**

Braiker, Harriet. *The Disease to Please: Curing the People-Pleasing Syndrome*. McGraw Hill Professional, 2002.

Cloud, Henry. *Necessary Endings: The Employees, Businesses, and Relationships That All of Us Have to Give Up in Order to Move Forward.* Harper Collins, 2011.

Cloud, Henry, and John Townsend. *Boundaries: When To Say Yes, How to Say No*. Zondervan, 2008.

Cloud, Henry. *Safe People: How to Find Relationships That Are Good for You and Avoid Those That Aren't*. Zondervan, 2009.

Cloud, Henry, and John Sims Townsend. *Boundaries: When to Say Yes, When to Say No to Take Control of Your Life*. 2003

Furtick, Steven. *Sun Stand Still Devotional: A Forty-Day Experience to Activate Your Faith*. Multnomah, 2013.

Guyon, Jeanne Marie Bouvier de La Motte. *Experiencing the Depths of Jesus Christ*. 1981.

Meyer, Joyce. *Approval Addiction*. Hachette UK, 2012.

Meyer, Joyce. *Battlefield of the Mind Bible: Renew Your Mind Through the Power of God's Word*. Hachette UK, 2017.

Meyer, Joyce. *The Everyday Life Bible: The Power of God's Word for Everyday Living*. Hachette UK, 2018

TerKeurst, Lysa. *Good Boundaries and Goodbyes: Loving Others Without Losing the Best of Who You Are*. 2022.

**Websites:**

http:// www.bibleu.academy

http://www.danielsden.com

http://www.elevationchurch.org

http://www.gatewaypeople.com

http://www.intouch.org

http://www.JoyceMeyer.org

http://www.KeionHenderson.com

http://www.lifechange.org

http://www.livingwatersministry.com

http://www.pastorrick.com

http://www.pottershouse.org

http://www.saddleback.com

https://tonyevans.org

Printed in Great Britain
by Amazon